General editor: Graham Handley MA Ph.D.

Brodie's Notes on Emily Brontë's

Wuthering Heights

Bill Nathan BA
Formerly English Master, Gowerton Comprehensive School

MACMILLAN

D0258400

First published 1990 by Pan Books Ltd

Published 1992 by
MACMILLAN PRESS LTD
Houndmills, Basingstoke, Hampshire RG21 6XS
and London
Companies and representatives
throughout the world

ISBN 0–333–58055–9

A catalogue record for this book is available
from the British Library.

This book is printed on paper suitable for recycling and
made from fully managed and sustained forest sources.

12 11 10 9 8 7 6
03 02 01 00 99 98

Printed in Great Britain by
Mackays of Chatham PLC
Chatham, Kent

Contents

Preface by the general editor

The intention throughout this study aid is to stimulate and guide, to encourage your involvement in the book, and to develop informed responses and a sure understanding of the main details.

Brodie's Notes provide a clear outline of the play or novel's plot, followed by act, scene, or chapter summaries and/or commentaries. These are designed to emphasize the most important literary and factual details. Poems, stories or non-fiction texts combine brief summary with critical commentary on individual aspects or common features of the genre being examined. Textual notes define what is difficult or obscure and emphasize literary qualities. Revision questions are set at appropriate points to test your ability to appreciate the prescribed book and to write accurately and relevantly about it.

In addition, each of these Notes includes a critical appreciation of the author's art. This covers such major elements as characterization, style, structure, setting and themes. Poems are examined technically – rhyme, rhythm, for instance. In fact, any important aspect of the prescribed work will be evaluated. The aim is to send you back to the text you are studying.

Each study aid concludes with a series of general questions which require a detailed knowledge of the book: some of these questions may invite comparison with other books, some will be suitable for coursework exercises, and some could be adapted to work you are doing on another book or books. Each study aid has been adapted to meet the needs of the current examination requirements. They provide a basic, individual and imaginative response to the work being studied, and it is hoped that they will stimulate you to acquire disciplined reading habits and critical fluency.

Graham Handley 1991

Page references are to the Pan Classics
edition of *Wuthering Heights* but references
are also given to particular chapters so that
the Notes may be used with any edition of the novel.

The author's life and works

Emily Brontë was born on 30 July 1818 at her father's parsonage at Thornton in the parish of Bradford, the fifth child in a family of six. In 1820 they moved to Haworth, where Mr Brontë had been appointed to a 'perpetual curacy'. The following year Mrs Brontë died and her sister Miss Elizabeth Branwell came from Cornwall to help Mr Brontë look after his large family. Unfortunately Aunt Branwell, conventional and strict, lacked insight into the emotional needs of small children. She did her best, teaching the girls sewing, household management and their 'duty', but she was no mother to the young family. Emily respected, but remained largely uninfluenced by, her aunt. However, Maria and Elizabeth, the two eldest children, were astonishingly protective and intelligent and did a great deal to generate an atmosphere of love and security. Kind servants too helped in this respect.

The Rev Patrick Brontë, Emily's father, though austere and busy, clearly did his best to compensate for the absence of a mother, but it seems that the children did suffer rather from his comparative lack of warmth and humour. These qualities they provided for themselves through their close inter-dependence. However, there can be no doubt that Mr Brontë had a beneficial influence on his children. He had always loved poetry, music, politics, the countryside, animals and walking; he encouraged Emily's natural interest in all these. He was certainly no ogre: later in life he respected Emily's unconventional religious views and made no effort to oblige her to teach in Sunday school.

The parsonage with its adjacent churchyard where Emily spent most of her short life was a somewhat forbidding home, but like Catherine Earnshaw in *Wuthering Heights* the young girl developed an intense love for the moorland environment which she never lost. Her favourite occupation was rambling on the heath with her brother and sisters or with only a dog as companion. Emily always valued freedom and independence, and her naturally reserved, introspective personality guarded these quiet passions. It is probable, too, that the character of the people of the area reinforced her reserve. Mrs Gaskell tells us in her *Life* that they were a 'lawless, yet not unkindly population, self-reliant, reserved, practical, earthy, suspicious of "foreigners", their accost . . . curt; their accent and tone of speech blunt and harsh . . .' Emily had little contact with the local villagers and rarely sought society, but she had been born and brought up in the influence of the West Riding and to some extent shared its qualities (like many of the characters in her novel).

In 1824 Mr Brontë sent Emily and Charlotte to Cowan Bridge School for the Daughters of Clergymen (reproduced in Charlotte's *Jane Eyre*). It was a dreadful experience for Charlotte, because her two elder sisters Maria and Elizabeth, also at Cowan Bridge, were taken home where they died of tuberculosis in consecutive months in 1825. Emily and her sister were also brought home. Charlotte and her brother Branwell were lastingly affected by this double tragedy; Emily, just six, appears to have been too young to have fully realized what had happened, but she must certainly have been affected by the grief of the rest of the household – her brother's insistence, for example, that he heard Maria crying outside the window is reflected in the episode in Chapter 3 of *Wuthering Heights* when Lockwood encounters the ghost of Catherine Earnshaw wailing to be let into her childhood room.

Back home in Haworth, Emily and the other children were left largely to themselves, and how they created their 'secret world' of fantasy is now a famous literary story. Their chief interest was in the creation of imaginary people, and they began, like all children, by improvising noisy plays. But they soon channelled this creative play into writing innumerable little books, some less than two inches square, in such Lilliputian handwriting that they could scarcely be read without the help of a magnifying glass. This fantasy world kept such an extraordinary hold over Emily in particular that it became an addiction, a form of escapism that was no doubt partly a substitute for real life. But it also led eventually to her mature lyric poetry, to her novel, and to her strong personal, mystical vision of life.

The origin of this imaginary world, according to Charlotte's History of the Year 1829, lay in a present from their father in 1826:

Papa bought Branwell some wooden soldiers at Leeds; when Papa came home it was night, and we were in bed, so next morning Branwell came to our door with a box of soldiers. Emily and I jumped out of bed, and I snatched one up and exclaimed, 'This is the Duke of Wellington! This is the Duke!' When I had said this, Emily likewise took up one and said it should be hers; when Anne came down, she said one should be hers.

The twelve soldiers became twelve young men who established the African kingdom of Great Glass Town, about which the children wrote an enormous number of histories, 'newspapers', magazines, and so on.

In 1831, when Charlotte went to Roe Head School, the children decided to destroy the Great Glass Town (Charlotte wrote a poem for the event). In Charlotte's absence, Emily and Anne invented a more important world, the Gondal saga, peopled with royal heroes and heroines, noble exiles and prisoners, and strongly influenced by Scott, the Border Ballads, and Byron's poetry and personality. The Gondal world produced many poems and stories, strengthening the intense inner life of the future writer of *Wuthering Heights*, shaping her development as a poet (and providing solace as late as 1837 when Emily was teaching at Law Hill School near Halifax and hating every minute of it). The picture evoked by her diary-paper of 24 November 1834, shows the importance to Emily of the Gondal fantasy. It was as real to her, in its way, as the domestic routine at the parsonage:

Taby said just now Come Anne pilloputate [peel a potato] Aunt has come into the kitchen just now and said where are your feet Anne — Anne answered On the floor Aunt. Papa opened the parlour door and gave Branwell a letter saying here Branwell read this and show it to your Aunt and Charlotte — The Gondals are discovering the interior of Gaaldine — Sally Mosley is washing in the back kitchen . . .

The children thus created this complex and deeply satisfying dream world together, Emily contributing as much as anyone and, indeed, often initiating ideas because of her strong imagination and sense of humour. Nevertheless, she remained very reserved, even in this play world, keeping to herself her most important personal feelings. Unlike her brother Branwell, Emily was never gregarious. Charlotte later said of her, 'My sister Emily was not a person of demonstrative character, nor one on the recesses of whose mind and feelings, even those nearest and dearest to her could, with impunity, intrude unlicensed.'

As well as writing stories and poems at this early age, Emily played the piano well and was a gifted artist; her drawings of birds and dogs are especially delicate. She was educated at home by her father at this time, and also by Charlotte when she returned from Roe Head. Emily was very intelligent, but she was not cut out for conventional academic studies and these were erratic. She much preferred a walk on the moors, often finding inspiration there for her poems.

In 1835 Charlotte returned to Roe Head as a teacher. Emily, now the tallest and most attractive of the sisters, went with her as pupil, for Mr Brontë was anxious to educate her as well as his small salary permitted. Unhappily, Emily developed such a strong sense of exile from her beloved moors and became so ill from homesickness that she was brought home after a mere three months. It is clear that the impact of school discipline and the loss of privacy and freedom, both literally vital to Emily, were intolerable. Her sister Anne went to school in her place but she too, chronically delicate, soon came home.

At this time of crisis Branwell too was unhappy: he had been unable to face the challenge of presenting himself for interview at the Royal Academy School, where he had hoped to study painting, and had squandered his money on drink. As his portrait of Emily in the National Portrait Gallery shows, he was a talented artist, and this moral failure was a severe blow to him and an acute disappointment to his father. From this time Branwell deteriorated, taking a series of jobs, mostly unsuitable, drinking excessively when he had the money, and taking opium, then cheap and easily obtainable.

Back at home and perfectly well again, Emily was happy. Free to roam the moors, made secure and amused by the well-loved servant 'Tabby', and living vicariously and intensely in the realms of Gondal, she was passing from girlhood into maturity as a mystic and lyrical poet, her true world. Here she was able to escape from domesticity, from the limitations of the body into a world where there was 'only spirit wandering wide/Through infinite immensity'. Her best poems of this time clearly reflect the beauty and intensity of her sense of fusion with Nature.

In 1837, motivated perhaps by the desire to prove herself capable of acting like Charlotte and Anne, both back at school, Emily took a teaching post at Law Hill School near Halifax. This was important, for it widened Emily's knowledge of people and gave her material she was to use ten years later in her novel. There were compensations, such as walking on the hills above the industrial town, but the work was oppressive to a young woman who valued solitude and quietness, and again the sense of exile was strong. She stayed only six months, returning to Haworth in June 1838, where she remained for the next four years, looking after her father, helping Branwell when and as she could, walking on the moors and writing poetry.

In 1842, falling in with Charlotte's idea that the three sisters should aim at having a school of their own, Emily accompanied Charlotte to Brussels to study at the *pensionnat* of Madame and Monsieur Heger, in order to improve their French and therefore their chances of success in the competitive world of private schools for young ladies (at this time of course there was no system of state education as we know it today). Study was less demanding than teaching, and this time Emily's health appears to have been stable, partly because of her sister's companionship. They worked hard, and life was tolerable, but we can deduce from Charlotte's letters that Emily's diligence was due to will-power, not contentment – she was not a social creature and it is impossible to imagine her happy anywhere away from her moors. In October Aunt Branwell died and the sisters came home; Charlotte later returned to Brussels, but Emily thankfully stayed at Haworth. With a small legacy from her aunt she was now more independent than ever before, and so, contented. In 1844 Charlotte finally left Brussels and came home, unhappy in unrequited love, but with renewed plans for her own school.

Charlotte eventually came to terms with her unhappy love affair, but Branwell could not cope with his unreturned love for Mrs Robinson, his employer's wife. Scandalously, in July 1845 he was dismissed from his post as tutor (and finally rejected by Mrs Robinson the following year after the death of her husband). He had also lost a previous job as a railway official, and was in debt. The Brontë family, united as always, helped Branwell with money that might have gone into the school project, which was now once more shelved. For the next four years, until his premature death in 1848, Branwell was constantly ill, struggling with his addiction to drink and opium, often suicidally unstable. Emily in particular tried to help him, possibly knowing her brother's mental state better than anyone; there are several stories about her helping him in his bouts of drunkenness. She once put out a fire started by Branwell in his bedroom while deeply drugged.

In the autumn of 1845 Charlotte accidentally found Emily's poems, read them, and at once recognized their power and originality – far greater than her own. Emily was furious at this violation of her privacy and it took Charlotte a long time to placate her and subsequently to persuade her sister to join her and Anne in the publication of a selection of their poems. This volume duly appeared in May 1846 as *Poems by Currer, Ellis and Acton Bell* – the sisters changed their names but kept their initials. The book had no commercial success, but Emily's poems were rightly singled out by an *Athenaeum* critic: he found in the verse of 'Ellis Bell' 'an evident power of wing', 'inspiration' and 'a fine quaint spirit'. Charlotte must have been pleased at this endorsement of her opinion of Emily's poems (see her 'Biographical Notice', pp. 21–3). The best of them, lyrics such as 'Cold in the earth', 'Enough of Thought, Philosopher', 'No coward soul is mine', 'O thy bright eyes', and 'The linnet in the rocky dells' are totally personal and underivative, and possess an intensity and clarity of mood and utterance that remind us of Blake and Wordsworth.

Not discouraged, the Brontë trio went on writing, and in due course they each produced a novel. Charlotte's *Jane Eyre*, Emily's *Wuthering Heights*, and Anne's *Agnes Grey* were all published in 1847. Anne's *The Tenant of Wildfell Hall* came out the following year, and Charlotte went on to publish *Shirley* (in which the heroine is to some extent based on Emily), *The Professor*, and *Villette*.

Emily's novel was not received with any enthusiasm; many of the reviewers were not so much hostile as mystified by the strangeness and originality of the characters and incidents. But on the whole its reception was not one likely to discourage its author from making a second attempt, and indeed there is some evidence that Emily began another novel. But now she fell ill. For some time she had been more than normally withdrawn and intractable; this may in part be ascribed to the failure of her poems and the lack of perceptive criticism of her novel. But it also seems likely, as Winifred Gérin suggests in her biography of Emily, that she was suffering from depression because of what appears to have been the loss of her poetic inspiration. She had also been greatly affected by the sadness of her sisters' futile love affairs, by their consequent ill-health, and by Branwell's last terrible illness and death in September 1848. A cold caught at her brother's funeral was neglected and on 19 December in the same year Emily died of pulmonary tuberculosis, the disease that killed all the Brontë children. She refused all medical aid until immediately before her death, and showed incredible courage and stoicism throughout the illness. It is possible, given all the circumstances, that she had lost the desire to live. The following year Anne died. Charlotte died at thirty-eight after a brief but happy marriage. Mr Brontë lived on to the age of eighty-four.

After a slow start, *Wuthering Heights* sold steadily throughout the nineteenth century – at first due, possibly, to the fascination exerted by the 'Bell' pseudonyms and its association with the more famous *Jane Eyre* – but then in its own right as a powerful and original story. Now it has been translated into many foreign languages; Sir Laurence Olivier starred as Heathcliff in a film version of the story; and it is one of the most famous of novels. And the Brontë family, one of the most famous of literary families, has made Haworth in Yorkshire almost as magnetic for pilgrims as is Stratford-on-Avon.

Plot, sources, setting and influences

Plot

Mr and Mrs Earnshaw lived in their farmhouse Wuthering Heights in the wild moorland countryside of Yorkshire with their two children Hindley and Catherine. One summer Mr Earnshaw walked to Liverpool and returned with an orphan of foreign appearance whom he had rescued from the streets of the port. He was determined to love and rear the boy as if he were his own son, and called the foundling Heathcliff, the name of a son who had died in childhood. At first all three children: Hindley, Catherine, and Ellen Dean (a servant girl who was almost one of the family), rejected Heathcliff. But soon only Hindley was antagonistic, regarding the newcomer as an interloper, usurping his place in his father's affections. Catherine, beautiful and spirited, felt a strong affinity for Heathcliff; very soon they were inseparable.

After Mr Earnshaw's death Hindley, now master of Wuthering Heights, sought revenge on Heathcliff. He rejected Heathcliff as an adopted brother, making him a servant – farm labourer and stable-boy – and humiliated and bullied him unmercifully. Heathcliff, stoical but very proud, would have run away had it not been for Catherine, whom he loved passionately. Catherine became friendly with Edgar Linton, the son of a rich neighbour and heir to Thrushcross Grange. One night Heathcliff overheard her tell Ellen that she had agreed to marry Edgar, because marriage with Heathcliff would degrade her. Heathcliff left before hearing Catherine add that she nevertheless loved Heathcliff deeply. He then disappeared for three years.

When he returned, Heathcliff found Catherine married to Edgar and mistress of Thrushcross Grange. He himself was now rich, mature, handsome, clearly a gentleman, though it was not known how this transformation had been effected. From now on Heathcliff's actions seemed governed largely by revenge. He settled at Wuthering Heights, partly to be near Catherine, partly to avenge himself on Hindley by encouraging him to drink and gamble: Heathcliff lent him money for this purpose. He also married Edgar's sister Isabella, who was infatuated with him, not because he loved her but because she was heiress to Edgar's property and also, perversely, because he hated her as she was a Linton. He treated her in an inhuman manner, knowing that this would hurt Edgar, whom he hated both because he was a Linton and because he had taken Catherine from him.

On Hindley's death, Heathcliff became the owner of Wuthering Heights, for it was mortgaged to him. Still in pursuit of revenge, he planned to degrade Hindley's son Hareton, as he had been degraded in his youth by Hindley. He insisted on staying in close contact with Catherine, and this led to the break-up of her marriage and, indirectly, to Catherine's illness and subsequent death on the birth of her daughter Cathy.

After Isabella's death, Heathcliff forced their son Linton to live with him at Wuthering Heights, knowing that this would be painful to Edgar for his sister's sake. He then terrorized Linton, who was chronically ill, into paying court to young Cathy Linton, and forced her to marry his son immediately before her father Edgar's death. Linton Heathcliff too died soon afterwards, so Heathcliff became master of Thrushcross Grange through his son, in case his claim through his late wife Isabella should prove illegal.

Heathcliff did not live for long after these events. He had always believed that Catherine's spirit haunted him, and now this obsession became so intense that ordinary life grew unreal. He died mysteriously, apparently because of failing to eat but really owing to the intensity of his desire to die in order to be reunited with Catherine. The story ends on a note of hope: Hareton, the real heir to Wuthering Heights, and Cathy, the true heiress to Thrushcross Grange, are in love and about to marry.

The following data about the two families may be useful:

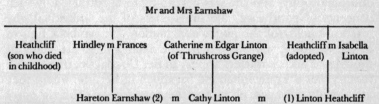

		Mr and Mrs Earnshaw		
Heathcliff (son who died in childhood)	Hindley m Frances	Catherine m Edgar Linton (of Thrushcross Grange)		Heathcliff m Isabella (adopted) Linton
	Hareton Earnshaw (2) m Cathy Linton m (1) Linton Heathcliff			

Hindley Earnshaw: Born 1757. Married 1777. Died September 1784.
Heathcliff: b. 1764. Brought to Wuthering Heights Summer 1771. m. January 1784. d. June 1802.
Catherine Earnshaw: b. Summer 1765. m. March 1783. d. 20 March 1784.

Edgar Linton: b. 1762. m. March 1783. d. Late August or early
September 1801.
Isabella Linton: b. Late 1765. m. January 1784. d. Summer 1797.
Cathy Linton: b. 20 March 1784. m. (1) August 1801. (2) Arranged for
1 January 1803.
Linton Heathcliff: b. September 1784. m. August 1801. d. Autumn
1801.
Hareton Earnshaw: b. June 1778. m. Arranged for 1 January 1803.

Sources

Wuthering Heights is a highly original novel, a powerful tale in the
Gothic manner but set in a familiar Yorkshire rather than an
exotic Italy or Germany. However (as we find also with many of
Shakespeare's plays), its narrative originality consists to some
extent in the writer's achievement in assimilating and reshaping
the miscellaneous material used – the literature she was steeped
in, her own experience, personality, and knowledge of life. All
these interacted, and Emily Brontë's imagination created an
artistic whole, a new world, out of a chaos of influences. Such a
process is a complex one, and it is not possible to trace every
episode or character to its origin. What we can usefully do is to
indicate the obvious sources of the basic plot, themes, and principal characters.

First, there are the literary sources. Emily was certainly a child
of her age, the Romantic era of Blake, Wordsworth, Coleridge,
Byron, Scott, Shelley and Keats. She was familiar with much of
this literature, available to her either in her father's study or
from the local library, and also with such journals as *Blackwood's
Magazine*, the *Leeds Intelligencer*, and *John Bull*. So from an early
age her mind was richly nourished by poetry, stories, politics,
and philosophy, and she was beginning to be attracted by such
concepts as pantheism, the uniqueness of the individual, the
mystical quality of the poetic imagination, the symbolic figures
of the explorer, the tragic hero, the exile, and so on. Many of
these ideas and characters appear in her Gondal poetry, the safe
fantasy world Emily inhabited for much of her life, where they
are already, perhaps, preparing the stage for the dramatic entry
of Heathcliff.

The figure of Satan in Milton's *Paradise Lost* had impressed
Emily, who may have felt an affinity for the fallen angel, powerful but thwarted, aware of the rights he has been deprived of, of

his lost goodness. This is one source of the satanic element in Heathcliff. Ballad poetry, too, stressed the idea of the hero: the Black Douglas of *Chevy Chase* and Scott's *The Lady of the Lake* have Heathcliffian features, and such ballads as the *Daemon Lover*, in which the human and the supernatural are blended, remind us of a similar fusion of the human and the devilish in Catherine Earnshaw's lover. Some ballads of this sort no doubt came to Emily from Tabby's songs, as well as via Percy's *Reliques* and Scott's *Border Minstrelsy*. Scott's novels certainly influenced Emily, as her Gondal poems show: they are full of Scottish names and topography. But whereas Scott regarded Nature as a picturesque background for 'derring-do', Emily Brontë had an intense personal feeling for Nature, with the result that in her novel the moorland setting is an organic part of the action, not just decorative background. Brontë's moors are integrated with the emotions and behaviour of her protagonists as Thomas Hardy's Egdon Heath is with Eustacia Vye, Clym Yeobright, and Venn the reddle-man. The moors are a source of atmosphere and mystical power, as are the landscapes in plays like *Lear* and *Macbeth*. Shakespeare, indeed, was a long-standing love and influence, and there is no doubt that his idea of the tragic hero, whether in the 'fallen angel' of devilish Macbeth, the royal Lear driven to madness, or the romantic Hotspur of *Henry IV, Part 1*, appealed strongly to Emily Brontë's imagination. Heathcliff is transformed by fate into a devil as powerful in his farmhouse as Macbeth in his castle.

The concept of the satanic hero may have come to Emily more directly from Byron than from any other single source. In Byron's verse tales like *Lara* and *The Giaour*, the Miltonic Satan figure develops other traits: he is defiant, anti-social, and his origins are hidden; he is associated with fatal love, a figure of doom, half man, half devil or god. The idea of possession by evil is prominent in the Gondal poems in the nature of the hero – a noble creature 'doomed to be/ Hell-like in heart and misery . . .'

The Gothic novel or terror tale, typified by such books as Mrs Radcliffe's *The Mysteries of Udolpho*, and very much in vogue in Emily's youth, inevitably influenced her. Many of the tales first appeared in *Blackwood's*, a magazine much in demand at Haworth. Winifred Gérin, in her biography of Emily, lists several books that contain ideas and characters similar to those in *Wuthering Heights*. There was Hoffman's *Devil's Elixir* (1824),

with its *doppelganger,* a man's double, an evil other self commit-
ting crimes abhorrent to the real self. The same idea was used in
James Hogg's *Confessions of a Justified Sinner,* which Emily certainly read; like *Wuthering Heights* the story has a realistic setting,
a plain prose style, a devil-possessed hero, grave-desecration, a
self-righteous servant, and a plot about inheritance –
allegorically the possession of a soul rather than the possession
of property.

Another book with material in common with Emily's novel was
Bartholomew Simmonds's *The Bridegroom of Barna,* which came
out in *Blackwood's* in 1840. Here too we find desecration of
graves, rival families, tragic love, a hero and heroine very similar
to Catherine and Heathcliff, general violence, and a central love
scene like that in *Wuthering Heights* (15, 168–73). It seems certain
that Emily read this book and that she drew upon it for some of
the detail of her novel. Similarly, Mary Shelley's *Valperga* uses
the idea of the alien identity, the good man transformed into an
evil one, a tyrant like Heathcliff with 'basilisk' eyes (the 'basilisk'
image also occurs in Byron's *The Giaour*). There can be little
doubt, too, that Emily read and was influenced by *Blackwood's*
translations from the works of the German Romantic Schiller –
Byronic ballads about injustice, avarice, and the isolated figure
of the poet-hero.

One of the most important features of the Gothic devil tale is
the non- or extra-human nature of the hero-villain. Charles
Maturin's *Melmoth the Wanderer* was one of the best known of
these stories, and it seems likely that this was one of the sources
for Heathcliff, whose bestial or inhuman element is stressed
throughout *Wuthering Heights* in such images as those invoked by
'cannibal', 'devil', 'basilisk', 'fiend', 'wolf', 'savage beast', and so
forth.

Setting and influences

All this, then, was the literary soil in which Emily's story so
readily germinated. But just as important, of course, was the
imprint of her own personality and experience. These cannot
always be disentangled from the complex effects of individual
books and the literary atmosphere of the time. Nevertheless,
some things are clear enough. In the first place, the writer's
strange, powerful personality is surely reflected in the originality

and power of the narrative. Emily's need for independence and freedom, her passion for the wild moorland, her inflexibility, unsociability, decisiveness and practical good sense – all these are mirrored in her book: in Catherine's passion for freedom and the moors, in Heathcliff's inflexibility and coldness to strangers. It is the Brontë sense of humour that gives life to Joseph's cynical jocularity and Heathcliff's vicious wit. Her sound business sense is reflected in the correct presentation of financial and legal matters. Her love of animals gives us the dogs at Wuthering Heights, and many of the animal references and images, though often illustrating violence, must remind us of the strong-minded woman who kept doves, cats, dogs, a merlin hawk and geese; the woman who was bitten by a mad dog she tried to befriend and promptly applied a red-hot iron to the wound; the mistress who dared to punish with her bare hands the savage house-dog Keeper and then bathed its bruised head – when Emily died it howled inconsolably for days outside her room.

Then there are the influences of Emily's family and their lives. From her father came tales of wild life in Ireland and Yorkshire, of the fanaticism of Methodists like William Grimshaw and Jabez Bunting, and of the violence of the Luddites. Echoes of these stories are loud in Joseph's savage bigotry, in Heathcliff's aggression, in Lockwood's religious nightmare, and whisper even in such details as Hindley's knife-gun – for Mr Brontë had a pistol for many years, and taught Emily to shoot. Similarly, Aunt Branwell's conventional strictness and her 'mad Methodist magazines' (Charlotte's phrase) contribute in some measure both to Joseph and to Ellen Dean. Here Emily's much-loved servant 'Tabby' has significance too: her homely humour and Yorkshire dialect connect her with Joseph's dialect and Ellen's matter-of-factness.

As we have seen, the idea of love as a doomed passion or a destructive force is a prominent feature of the Gothic tale. Love for Emily Brontë, it seems probable, was largely sublimated into poetry and nature mysticism, but her attitude was also affected by her observation of the destructive impact of unrequited love on her sisters Anne and Charlotte and on Branwell too (see 'Author's life', pp.11–12). All this is reflected, it may be argued, in the unhappiness of several of the love relationships in the novel. Unfulfilled love in Heathcliff leads to hate and vengeance and is a cause of Catherine's unhappiness and death. Grief for lost love transforms Hindley's energy into self-destruction. Mis-marriage destroys Isabella's happiness. The forced union of Cathy and Linton is the product of hatred and avarice. Only Hareton and Cathy have some hope of contentment from their love.

There is much illness and death in *Wuthering Heights*. Apart from the central and all-important death of Catherine Earnshaw, there are many references to deaths, declines, chronic delicacy, consumption, and so on. Old Mr and Mrs Earnshaw die early in the story; fever despatches Mr and Mrs Linton; poor Frances dies very movingly (8,88); Edgar fades pathetically away, wanting only reunion with Catherine. Isabella also dies of tuberculosis, and conceivably passes it on to her son, who dies of it just after his marriage. It is hard not to see behind this disease and mortality not only Emily's own attitude to death, which was essentially that of her heroine Catherine (see 15,171), but also the dim sadness of the deaths of her sisters Maria and Elizabeth, her brother's premature death and that of William Weightman with whom Anne had been secretly in love. It is really not surprising that death plays so large a part in Emily's sombre story.

Branwell of course has left his mark on *Wuthering Heights* in other ways. His personality, his addiction to alcohol, his physical and moral deterioration remind us of Hindley's dissipation and crack-up after the death of his wife. Also, Branwell's association with the Byronic 'doomed boy' and outcast of Emily's Gondal poems makes it likely that he contributes something to the shaping of Heathcliff. In this connection we might also note that the 'gypsy brat' Mr Earnshaw takes from the streets of Liverpool is very probably linked with the publicity given to the starving children of Irish immigrants in the port. Branwell had gone to Liverpool in 1845, just before Emily is thought to have started her novel, and could have given his sister an eye-witness report. As Winifred Gérin suggests, Heathcliff the child was no doubt of Irish extraction, and the 'gibberish' he spoke was Erse (Irish Gaelic).

Given Emily's passion for her West Riding moors, it is clear that the source of the few square miles of windswept heath that provide the setting for her story is the moorland environment of Haworth parsonage. Wuthering Heights is modelled chiefly on the farmstead at Top Withins, a few miles from Haworth, but includes some features of Law Hill House, near Halifax – a sombre, solid stone house. It is also thought that High Sunderland Hall, an impressive building Emily seems to have frequently walked to while teaching at Law Hill school, provided further detail for *Wuthering Heights*. Thrushcross Grange is usually identified with Ponden Hall, a few miles from Haworth, though this Hall is a much more modest building than Edgar Linton's Grange. Penistone Crag and its fairy cave are Ponden Kirk, the hollow towering rock in Ponden valley.

As has already been said (see 'Author's Life', p.10), Emily developed a mystical attachment for the moorlands around Haworth, and this binds her closely to her heroine Catherine, whose feeling for nature is similar. This mysticism influences the whole of the novel through the spiritual qualities it breathes into the setting. There can be few works of fiction more deeply rooted in an actual locality than *Wuthering Heights*.

Probably the most important source of all was a by-product of Emily's spell of teaching at Law Hill school, near Halifax, only eight miles from Haworth. Brussels seems to have contributed little to the novel, but Halifax gave the author the story of Jack Sharp. It is likely that she learned the history of Law Hill house from the school itself. Briefly, the story, well known in the area, was that a Mr Walker of Walterclough Hall (the same initials as Wuthering Heights, notice) adopted an orphan nephew, Jack Sharp. Owing to favouritism, he became arrogant. After his benefactor's death, he had to leave the Hall. But he built his own house at Law Hill and avenged himself on John Walker, the son and heir, by leaving Walterclough in a dilapidated state, by general malice, and by corrupting through gambling and drink a young relation of Walker's. The parallels here with the plot of Emily's story are clear; and there are other similarities: Sharp's manservant Joseph, and a children's nurse quite like Ellen Dean, for example.

There is little doubt that these ideas about adoption, property, ingratitude, inheritance, vindictiveness, and avarice, together with the central figure of the malicious 'cuckoo' Sharp, lay dormant in Emily's mind for nearly ten years before emerging in the main plot of *Wuthering Heights* and in the character of Heathcliff. But Brontë's imagination, working on the Sharp story and simultaneously on many other ideas from the various sources already suggested, recycles the material and transforms it into the stuff of tragedy. Her masterstroke, as her biographer Gérin notes, was to add the element of love to the mixture, first through the innocent love of the young Catherine and Heathcliff, then in the stormy passions of the figures in the 'eternal triangle', love tragically turned into hate, revenge, evil, and death by misuse. So the squalor of the Jack Sharp saga is replaced by a poetic romance with protagonists of almost Shakespearean stature.

In various forms these protagonists already existed, of course, before the impact of the Sharp story: as we have seen, Emily's reading had given her Byronic hero-villains and the familiar themes of tragic love, isolation, injustice, corruption, and so on. After her Law Hill period, partly because of her unhappiness there, the poetic impulse grew stronger and her mystical inner life more intense. There are numerous images and figures that look directly forward to *Wuthering Heights*: the 'iron man', 'the accursed man shut from his Maker's smile' (but redeemable through love), the tragic love of Fernando for the perfidious Augusta (her two sorts of lover correspond closely to the weak Edgar and the strong Heathcliff), and so forth. In the Gondal poems of, for example, the 1843–5 period, the familiar themes of union, alienation, the 'oneness' of life, the immortality of the spirit, the agony of love, the desire to be drawn into the soul of Nature, are found also in the novel. There the mysticism, poetry, and influences of all kinds fuse and flower with tragic brilliance in the story of the love of Heathcliff and Catherine – a human love that is also perhaps a symbol of the spiritual experience Emily sought and sometimes found in nature.

Chapter summaries, critical comment, textual notes and revision questions

Chapter 1

1801 – Mr Lockwood, the new tenant of Thrushcross Grange, describes his first visit to his landlord, Mr Heathcliff of Wuthering Heights. He is received inhospitably and his efforts to be sociable fail. Attacked by the house-dogs, he is saved by the intervention of the housekeeper. Heathcliff shows no sympathy, but when his tenant is indignant he becomes more amiable. They talk a little, then Lockwood leaves, resolving to pay another visit, though Heathcliff obviously does not want him to.

Commentary

Perhaps the first thing to strike the reader is the strength, clarity, and forthright manner of Emily Brontë's narrative method. The description of Lockwood and Heathcliff is lucid and deft, the writer establishing their personalities with a scrap of dialogue and imaginative detail. Two other characters, Joseph the man-servant, and the housekeeper, also come rapidly alive through graphic, humorous detail. Heathcliff is clearly the dominant figure: Byronically handsome, potentially violent, mysterious. Why is he so bad-tempered? Has he always been like this? Is he hiding something?

These narrative elements suggesting strangeness, conflict, the abuse of physical and social power, are both explicit and implicit. They are explicit in Heathcliff's suspicion of strangers, in Joseph's sour aloofness, in the aggressive guard-dogs. They are implicit in the nature of Wuthering Heights itself – its brutally exposed site, its sombre atmosphere suggesting even at this early stage in the story the possibility of dreadful happenings. The symbolism of the house reflects and reinforces the violent attitudes of the creatures it harbours.

It is noteworthy that this strangeness and violence are paralleled by what is ordinary, familiar, and friendly: the carefully described dresser, the unseen kitchen, the meat, the 'lusty dame' wielding a frying-pan, the glass of wine, the occasional good humour of the owner. This process of parallelism or juxtaposition is a constant feature of the book. The function of the familiar is to help the reader accept incredible people or events by encouraging what Coleridge called 'the willing suspension of disbelief' – if this suspension is difficult then the narrative illusion will be difficult to maintain. It is obviously the author's task so to engage the imagination of the reader or listener that his story is believed, at least while it is being told.

Other qualities noticeable in this chapter are the fluency of the prose style, the precision of the vocabulary (the student may feel that simpler words should sometimes be used), the elegance and harmony of the sentence construction, the easy but forceful tone of the narrative prose. 'Good prose,' said George Orwell, 'is like a window pane.' The window Emily Brontë invites us to look through is very clear: we see at once what she is pointing to, and the detail is sharp. Lockwood's first-person narration is also helpful to the reader in its suggestion of frankness and first-hand experience.

Note: d. = dialect.
arch = archaic language.

Wuthering Blustering, shaking, stormy (d.). See text, p.36.
griffins Fabulous monsters, part eagles, part lions.
shameless i.e. naked, but not ashamed of it.
date . . . Earnshaw Ponden Hall (see 'Setting and influences', p.21) has a similar inscription. The last date on the inscription above the entrance of the Hall is 1801, when the story begins.
penetralium Innermost shrine or recess.
underdrawn Inadequately revealed.
'never told my love' A quotation from Shakespeare's *Twelfth Night* (11.iv.109). Viola is speaking, and the actual words are 'never told *her* love . . .'
vis-à-vis Facing, opposite (Fr.).
The herd of possessed swine See the Bible, Matthew, 8,30–32, Mark, 5,11–13, Luke, 8,30–33. This reference to the devil-possessed Gadarene swine appropriately stresses the devilish nature of the house-dogs. Biblical allusions were more widely understood at the time *Wuthering Heights* was written.
signet i.e. trade-mark or, in other words, 'I should have left the marks of my fist on him.'

Chapter 2

When Lockwood returns to Wuthering Heights the following

day he is again rudely received, almost failing to gain admittance. He meets a young man and a younger woman, and after making embarrassing errors learns they are Hareton Earnshaw and Heathcliff's daughter-in-law, and that Heathcliff's wife and son are both dead. Lockwood's request for a guide to take him home through the blizzard is ignored, and when he starts to leave in disgust the dogs attack him once more. Again the housekeeper intervenes to help him. Since he has been badly upset he is forced to stay the night; Zillah, the housekeeper, shows him to a bed-chamber.

Commentary

The most interesting aspect of this chapter, not surprisingly, is the expansion of character interest. Heathcliff now more than ever dominates the action by his tyranny – his savage attitude towards his daughter-in-law makes Lockwood realize that his landlord is not the 'capital fellow' he first thought him but a man of 'genuine bad nature'. Subsequent indignities suffered by the tenant confirm this feeling. Heathcliff's nature is given more depth, and his mysterious appeal increases.

Joseph too becomes more alive, his dialect speech implying various qualities – pugnacity, unhelpfulness, religiosity; at times the West Riding speech suggests that he may turn out to be a stage-Yorkshireman, but there is no immediate danger of this. Indeed, the faithful transcription of the dialect indicates that he is more likely to contribute to the vital 'suspension of disbelief' by virtue of the homeliness of his talk (but as an unpleasant person he also contributes to the motif of inhospitability).

Two new characters emerge powerfully now – the young widow and Hareton. The writer establishes their salient features in direct, sparing description and in dialogue. Zillah reappears, partly for comic relief, but also to contribute to the motif of domesticity and ordinariness. Lockwood himself gains interest as we learn more about him; his social clumsiness is also a device for giving the reader important information in a reasonably natural manner. The narrator's polite conversation (comically incongruous in such a household) is the vehicle for some irony directed at 'polite society', but satire is not the main concern of the narrative.

The motif of zenophobia (note that strangers are to this day called 'foreigners' in parts of Yorkshire) is sustained throughout the chapter, in the attitudes of everyone in the house (except Zillah) towards the unlucky Lockwood, in the reserve or bad temper they also show to each other, and conspicuously in Heathcliff. As in the first chapter, the weather and the dogs are deployed to consolidate this process of hostility, and its dramatic climax is Lockwood's helpless rage and nose-bleed, the latter, forcing the visitor to stay the night, largely a device to develop the action, as we discover in the next chapter.

T' For 'the' in the dialect of the West Riding of Yorkshire.
fowld Fold, sheep enclosure or pen (d.).
laith Barn (d.).
flaysome Fearful, frightful (d.).
Aw'll . . . 't I'll have no hand in it (d.).
the door . . . attendance i.e. I had to knock on it so loudly.
hemmed i.e. made a 'hem' with my voice (indicating embarrassment or doubt).
Juno i.e. the pointer bitch. A suitable name for a guard-dog, as Juno in classical mythology was queen of heaven and one of the guardians of the state.
discussed Had, ate, consumed (arch.).
clown Peasant (arch.).
faishion Dare (d.).
nowt Nobody, good-for-nothing (d.).
Black Art Witchcraft.
postern Door leading outside, back door or gate.
copestone i.e. finishing touch. The cope-stone is the head stone of a building.
smacked of King Lear A reference to the bitter fury of King Lear (in Shakespeare's play of that name) towards Cordelia, his favourite daughter, when honesty prevented her from giving her father a declaration of total love.
agait Going on, afoot (d.).

Chapter 3

The closet-bed in the room where Lockwood spends the night encloses a window ledge holding mildewed books and scratched with the names *Catherine Earnshaw, Catherine Heathcliff, Catherine Linton.* He finds some of Catherine Earnshaw's books and part of her diary written on the spaces in these. He sleeps badly, having nightmares, in one of which he breaks the glass of a window and has his hand seized by that of the ghost of Catherine Linton, who pleads to be let in. His horrified screams bring in Heathcliff, who is angry and upset by Lockwood's presence in that particular room. He tells his host about the spectre in his dream and then is amazed to see Heathcliff opening the window to beseech the ghost to come to him (it does not).

Lockwood spends the rest of the night downstairs, until the household rises at four. He declines breakfast, then Heathcliff accompanies him back to the gates of Thrushcross Grange, two miles from the house itself.

Commentary

In this chapter we are brought nearer the central story, still via the narrator Lockwood, who is taken to the mysterious bedroom (Heathcliff 'had an odd notion about the chamber' but of course we are not told why). The closet-bed, which plays an important part in the story, is described in vivid detail, and Lockwood's discovery of the scratched names is a kind of anticipatory synopsis of the plot in its reference to the heroine and her daughter: Heathcliff's Cathy is first Catherine Earnshaw, who marries and becomes Catherine Linton. Her daughter, also Catherine Linton, marries Heathcliff's son and so becomes Catherine Heathcliff, but is to remarry her cousin and so become Catherine Earnshaw – the wheel turning full cycle. But more realistically, it would be typical of a young girl in love to practise what she hopes may one day be her married name.

The discovery of the diary is important, partly because like all diaries it is interesting for its own sake and also because it heralds an immediate change of narrator. The next two pages are autobiographical in style and are devoted to a direct, dramatic evocation of the past (juxtaposed to Lockwood's present). A typical Sunday at Wuthering Heights is described when the young Cathy and Heathcliff were suffering from Joseph's religious tyranny (see p.50), and Hindley's tyranny as master ('I wish my father were back again. Hindley is a detestable substitute . . .,' writes Cathy). The use of dialect to register Joseph's wrath and moral indignation is both comic and dramatic (p.51), and the diary extract ends by suggestively pinpointing Cathy's favourite occupation, 'a scamper on the moors', and her companion's new, degraded status.

The next section, dealing with the religious nightmare

(pp.52–54), does not advance the action, but it emphasizes Joseph's religiosity, and reflects Emily Brontë's ironic views on the excesses of Yorkshire Methodism and the irrelevance of organized religion – she believed religion was a private matter. The nightmare in the chapel neatly and realistically switches to the nightmare in the bedroom, via the link of the tapping branch. The ensuing ghost sequence is handled brilliantly, the detail evoking dream horror: the 'ice-cold hand', the blood from the cruel laceration, the ghost's face and 'doleful cry', the feeling that it is actually happening. The writer's skill is also clear when she makes dream and reality merge: Heathcliff's entry and emotional appeal to Cathy's ghost (pp.57-8). This is compulsive narrative, deepening the mystery enveloping Heathcliff, intensifying suspense. If this is melodrama, it is poetic in its force. The whole of this scene is expertly handled: the feelings evoked sharply, the atmosphere electric, description dramatically visualized.

clothes-press A large clothes-cupboard, normally with shelves.
lugs Ears (d.).
laiking Playing (d.).
scroop Back cover of a book (d.).
pawsed his fit Pushed his finger (or fist, possibly) (d.).
flaysome See note p.26.
gait Way (d.) cf. 'agait', note p.26.
laced Thrashed (d.).
'Seventy Times Seven' See Matthew 18,21–22.
determine into i.e. end as (become), through neglect.
four hundred and ninety i.e. seventy times seven.
sconces Skulls (arch.).
Grimalkin A common name for an old or grey cat, usually female.

Chapter 4

At her employer's request, Mrs Dean, the housekeeper, tells him Heathcliff's history.

He was a foundling brought home from Liverpool by Mr Earnshaw of Wuthering Heights, to be reared as his own son; he was given the name 'Heathcliff. Mr Earnshaw loved the boy, and soon his daughter Catherine did too, but her brother Hindley did not get over his resentment and regarded the newcomer as an interloper. Ellen Dean, then a servant-girl at the Heights but almost one of the family, softened in her attitude to

Heathcliff, but did not like him greatly. Since Mr Earnshaw made the boy his favourite, Heathcliff 'bred bad feeling'. Hindley continued to hate his adopted brother, bullying him viciously. Heathcliff endured this treatment quietly, but he knew how Mr Earnshaw loved him and would coolly use this love, which he showed no sign of returning, to get what he wanted.

This chapter contains a description of Heathcliff as a boy.

Commentary

The first section of this chapter, mainly duologue between Lockwood and Mrs Dean, serves two purposes: first, it forms the transition from Lockwood's narrative to the much more important story to be told by Mrs Dean. Secondly, it is another acceptable device for providing information rapidly and directly. This opening section is interesting stylistically too because of the nature of the imagery used – mainly in similes – to expand our insight into the enigma called Heathcliff: 'Rough as a saw-edge, and hard as whinstone!' and 'Hareton . . . cast out like an unfledged dunnock!' (pp.62–63). But the 'cuckoo' metaphor (p.63) is of central importance because it illustrates and dramatizes one of Heathcliff's roles in the plot – that of the tyrant and usurper, displacing Hindley and others, as a cuckoo displaces eggs and fledglings from the nest of the foster-parents. (But note that Heathcliff too suffers usurpation: the gentle Edgar and his social allure deprive him of the only thing he ever truly wanted – Catherine.) This metaphor is one of a series of figures of speech organically related to the story through their reference to character, event, theme, or setting.

Mrs Dean's narrative begins (p.63) with the beguiling simplicity of magical story-telling: how Mr Earnshaw walks to Liverpool, one hundred and twenty miles there and back in three days, and brings not the expected gifts but the dubious substitute, 'a dirty, ragged, black-haired child'. The lost whip and crushed fiddle may perhaps be regarded as symbols relating to the 'cuckoo' displacement motif. The children's expectation and its anti-climax are very well handled, as is the automatic rejection of the 'foreigner', childishly blamed for the loss of the presents. This rejection, an important lever in the plot, is convincing – Nelly's action in putting the 'gypsy brat' 'on the landing of the stairs, hoping it (note 'it') might be gone by the morrow' is especially imaginative and true to life. Note that because the 'poor, fatherless child' is given the name of a son who died young, there is no mistaking Mr Earnshaw's intentions.

indigenae Natives (Lat.).
whinstone Hard sandstone.
dunnock Hedge-sparrow.
the three kingdoms England, Scotland and Wales.
flighted Scolded, harassed (d.).
now very thick close.

Revision questions on Chapters 1–4

1 Describe Lockwood's first visit to Wuthering Heights.

2 Give a detailed description of Heathcliff, the farmhouse he lives in, and the other members of the household.

3 Give a detailed account of Lockwood's nightmarish experiences during his second visit to the Heights.

4 What do we learn of Ellen Dean (a) as a child and (b) as Lockwood's housekeeper?

5 Describe Heathcliff as a child. How did he come to be at Wuthering Heights, and how was he received there?

Chapter 5

Mr Earnshaw's health began to fail. The atmosphere at home became worse, owing to Hindley's continuing antagonism to Heathcliff, but improved when Hindley was sent away to college. However, Catherine, attractive but mischievous, worried her father a great deal. Joseph encouraged him to discipline both her and Heathcliff, and also gained influence over his employer by persuading him of the need to seek salvation through moral purity. Heathcliff, knowing how Catherine loved him, would always do what she wanted, even if this made Mr Earnshaw angry or anxious. At last Mr Earnshaw died, quietly one evening. Sadness brought Catherine and Heathcliff even closer together.

This chapter contains a description of Catherine as a girl.

Commentary

This short chapter contains several developments, all controlled with typical conciseness and clarity of style. The characterization of Heathcliff expands, in accordance with the paradox that 'a favourite has no friend': Mr Earnshaw thinks that because he favours the orphan, everyone else hates and resents him. This is not wholly the case, for Catherine loves Heathcliff, but such hatred and resentment is found importantly in Hindley. The tension caused by these destructive emotions is partly relieved when Hindley is sent off to college. Note that Ellen's efforts to humour the adopted son as Earnshaw wishes was 'rich nourishment to the child's pride and black tempers' – these elements in the hero-villain's nature are present throughout the novel. Here we have an account of their origin in the psychological tensions set up in the character because of the interaction in his mind of insecurity and expectation.

The removal of the main source of hatred and resentment leaves a narrative vacuum for the moment that is at once filled by another – Joseph's religious despotism. This affects all the other members of the household, particularly the master and the children (see p.68). The author's irony, via Ellen's opinions, at the expense of religious bigotry and self-righteousness, is clear and cogent.

The description of Catherine (pp.68–9) stresses her vitality and wildness. 'A wild, wicked slip', her impulsive sense of humour often results in misdirected vitality, as when she teased her father. And her sense of fun sometimes goes with irresponsibility: she is not sensitive enough about her father's unsatisfied need to be loved by Heathcliff. Our heroine is by no means perfect, though at this stage perhaps the hero feels she is. But it is likely that this makes her a more credible character.

The characters all become more vivid through the description of the domestic tensions. The climax of the death at the end of the chapter is skilfully contrived: for once Catherine is behaving herself, her father is pleased and tranquil. The scene has much atmosphere: everyone 'as mute as mice' (a typical narrator's simile, simple and domestic), the high wind blustering round the house and 'roaring in the chimney' (Wuthering Heights living up to its name in this crisis), Catherine singing gently and for some time unaware that her father has died.

Pharisee i.e. hypocrite. A Pharisee was a member of an ancient Jewish
   sect notorious for excessive ritual and legal strictness, and hence
   self-righteousness.
shopping A misprint for 'slapping'.
rarely Greatly.
frame Go (d.).

Chapter 6

Hindley came home to his father's funeral, surprisingly bringing
a wife – a somewhat silly if pretty girl. Now master at Wuthering
Heights, Hindley promptly reorganized affairs to suit himself:
he banished Ellen and Joseph to the back-kitchen, was tyrannically strict to his sister, and ignored his father's clear wishes by
making Heathcliff a servant – stable-hand and field labourer –
and depriving him of education. Punishment for both Catherine
and Heathcliff was frequent and severe. In response to this
tyranny, they became even more inseparable, often spending
their free time on the moors together. One Sunday evening, sent
out of the sitting-room for some minor offence, they went out
on the moor and, seeing the lights of Thrushcross Grange, ran
there to spy for fun on the Lintons through the window, to see
what *their* Sunday evenings were like. Unfortunately, they were
discovered; they ran off, but a bull-dog seized Catherine by the
ankle, and they were caught and taken inside. At first they were
thought to be thieves, but when they were recognized, Catherine
was tenderly cared for; Heathcliff was sent away, for they looked
upon him as socially inferior.

   Hindley was furious about this escapade, and when old Mr
Linton came and condemned him for not looking after his sister
properly, this anger was aggravated. Consequently, he threatened to dismiss Heathcliff if he so much as spoke to Catherine.

Commentary

Frances's peevish dislike of Heathcliff now leads (see p.72) to the
important description of the life led by the 'unfriended creatures', Catherine and Heathcliff, in the shadow of Hindley's
dictatorship – a life that contrasts effectively with the way they
lived when old Earnshaw was in charge. The motif of vengeance
of course centres on the methodical degradation of the adopted
son, the refusal to recognize him as such. Hindley's revenge in

turn fortifies pride and the desire for revenge in Heathcliff, and also drives brother and sister further apart, for Catherine always takes Heathcliff's side.

Characteristically, Emily Brontë dramatizes these emotions and the life of the outcast children, by means of the Thrushcross Grange incident. This is done almost entirely through Heathcliff's monologue (see pp.73–6), which has a wealth of narrative detail.

Technically, of course, the episode is crucial, for in it is the beginning of Catherine's 'social seduction' by the luxury and upper-class values of the Lintons: the climax of the incident heralds the chief crisis in the relationship of Heathcliff and his Cathy – old Linton's reaction reinforces Hindley's wish to keep the lovers apart and get rid of the 'interloper'. Thus the strong natural love of the two main characters is threatened by the strong 'unnatural' force of social ambition. Cathy's impending transformation is obviously, therefore, a powerful incentive for us to carry on reading.

catechised Questioned systematically (for the purpose of religious instruction). A catechism was a manual of religious instruction in dialogue form.
cant Talk hypocritically (especially of moral or religious matters).
pendent Usually 'pendant' – hanging, drooping.
Lascar East Indian sailor.
negus A hot mixture of wine and water, flavoured and sweetened.

Chapter 7

'Cathy stayed at Thrushcross Grange five weeks', and came back on Christmas Eve, looking quite a lady. Heathcliff was abashed in her presence, for the contrast in their appearance was now marked; and Frances hoped to complete the 'reforming' of Catherine begun at the Grange by means of 'fine clothes and flattery'. Heathcliff, now just a servant, had been much neglected during Catherine's absence.

The Lintons were invited to spend Christmas day at Wuthering Heights as an acknowledgement of their kindness to Catherine. Heathcliff was kept in the background (at Mrs Linton's request), but after Ellen had persuaded him to swallow his pride and make an effort, he made an appearance, clean and well-dressed. But Hindley's contempt led to an incident in which

Heathcliff threw hot sauce in Edgar's face after the latter insulted him. Hindley thrashed Heathcliff and locked him up in the garret for the rest of the day. Catherine was unhappy, angry with Edgar and sorrowing for Heathcliff. During a dance in the evening she let him out, and he sat in the kitchen thinking about how to get his revenge on Hindley.

Mrs Dean stops telling her story, as it is getting late, but Lockwood persuades her to go on.

Commentary

The first paragraph contains the ominous picture of the returning Catherine: the pony and the splendid clothes symbolize the social impact of the Lintons and lead on to the visual contrast between Cathy and the dirty, badly-dressed Heathcliff (pp.78–9). The latter's humiliation stresses the gap that now exists between the two, a gap that is widened when the Lintons visit, because the 'naughty, swearing boy' is kept away from them. The description of the solitary Nelly is good narrative, contributes to the motif of domesticity, and also leads on to her attempt to help Heathcliff, both for his own sake and because of her sad memory of her dead master and his hopes for his adopted son.

The dialogue, eventually showing the growth of hope in Heathcliff, is also the means by which the novelist is preparing to dash her hero's hopes. Now, ironically because of his decent clothes, he suffers humiliation again from Hindley, who accuses him of 'attempting the coxcomb', and the weakness of his pride and fiery temper leads to the inevitable assault on Edgar – a good example of his violent nature. It is noteworthy that in this crisis Catherine blames Edgar, whose insult provokes the quarrel.

This hope for Heathcliff is strengthened by means of Cathy's hidden sorrow at the feast and later when she goes to Heathcliff in the garret and Nelly 'let the poor things converse unmolested'. But hope is not encouraged by the climax of this episode, which is Heathcliff's declaration of his intention to get his revenge on his persecutor no matter how long he has to wait. We have the uneasy feeling that vengeance might become more important to the hero than love.

beaver Hat made of beaver fur.
cant Cheerful, brisk (d.).
His cake i.e. Heathcliff's.
Gimmerton band The rural custom of the village band visiting the
  principal houses of the district at Christmas time was widespread.
glees Part-songs.
'devil's psalmody' Many strict religious sects thought singing and
  dancing evil.

Chapter 8

Hindley's wife gave birth to a healthy son (Hareton), but died of
consumption quite soon afterwards. The baby became Ellen's
responsibility. Hindley's grief drove him into bitterness and
despair, and thence to dissipation; he found further relief in
treating Heathcliff badly. The latter was pleased to witness
Hindley's dissipated state because he hated the man. Because of
Hindley's reputation, 'nobody decent' came to the house now,
except Edgar Linton. Catherine seemed to be attracted by
Edgar, but she was also strongly attached to Heathcliff, and this
double life made matters difficult for her. On one of Linton's
visits (contrived in the absence of Hindley), the tension in her
led to a display of violent temper that shocked Edgar: he was at
first inclined to leave and perhaps see her no more, but love was
too strong – the quarrel simply 'effected a closer intimacy', and
made them 'confess themselves lovers'.

Commentary

The revenge theme developed through Heathcliff's meditation
on vengeance noted at the end of the previous chapter (see p.85)
is not immediately resumed, but the new chapter opens well in
the traditional 'One fine day' manner. We are now about to be
presented with the realities of rural life theoretically admired by
Lockwood (p.86). Accordingly, Hindley's son, born of love,
comes safely into the world, but his mother Frances, that 'mere
rush of a lass', dies.

Grief is now a lever to move the story on: Hindley, in despair,
grows to hate God and his fellow-men; there is much hate in the
novel, most of it in Heathcliff and Hindley. Wuthering Heights
becomes 'an infernal house', with its resident devils Earnshaw,
Heathcliff (and perhaps even the nasty Joseph, in spite of his

religion). Drink and gambling rear their ugly heads, the servants leave, though not the loyal Nelly, nor Joseph, 'because it was his vocation to be where he had plenty of wickedness to reprove' (p.89). The hero-villain's pride and 'savage sullenness and ferocity' increase, as does his appetite for vengeance – it is already being whetted by Hindley's rapid deterioration. Only Edgar comes to the house now, to see Catherine, 'queen of the countryside'. The digression concerned with Edgar's portrait is of course related to the main narrative, and it seems obtrusive even if it does momentarily induce suspense (p.89).

The detailed account of Catherine's 'double character', an important contribution to her characterization, stresses the tension created in her by conflicting desires – social ambition and Edgar on one hand, Heathcliff on the other. (This tension later becomes a major source of feeling and incident, as will be seen.)

The discontentment of the two main characters moves towards the scene in which Edgar will win her, but before this crisis we should note the formal similes used to sharpen the contrast between the two suitors and to herald the critical quarrel and love scene: Heathcliff is compared with a 'bleak, hilly, coal country', while Edgar is like a 'beautiful, fertile valley' (p.92).

Kenneth The village doctor.
foster-sister Her mother had been wet-nurse to Hindley (see 4, 63).
hers has been removed See 29, 278.
imposed Favourably impressed.
plate Metal domestic utensils.
naughty Arrogant, wicked, rather than mischievous – a modern meaning.

Chapter 9

After the accident in which Hareton was almost killed owing to his father's drunken behaviour, Ellen talked to Catherine in the kitchen. Edgar Linton had proposed, and she had accepted him, though with misgivings because she loved Heathcliff. Wishing to be reassured that she had acted for the best in agreeing to marry Edgar, Catherine told this to Ellen. Heathcliff was in the kitchen, unknown to the talkers, and overheard part of what Catherine was saying, notably that marriage with him would degrade her – at that point he slipped out. The rest of Catherine's statement, making clear how deeply and passionately she loved Heathcliff, and that her marriage to Edgar was really to help the former escape from Hindley's power, he did not hear.

Catherine, knowing from Ellen that Heathcliff had heard part of their conversation and frightened of what he might do, went out to find him, but could not. She stayed outside watching for him, in spite of a storm, and came in drenched and exhausted. She remained in this state all night, and in the morning was clearly ill with fever. Catherine recovered, convalescing at the Grange, but Mr and Mrs Linton both caught the fever and died.

Three years later (Heathcliff had never reappeared) she married Edgar and went to live at Thrushcross Grange. Ellen had to go with her, reluctantly parting from Hareton.

Commentary

The chapter seems to fall into three sections: the first implements the motif of violence in various ways. There is Hindley's drunken violence, potentially murderous, expressing itself largely in verbal aggression and in the gun and knife business. His love-hate attitude to the child Hareton, a see-saw of drunken emotion, leads directly to the dramatic moment when the boy falls from Hindley's arms and is caught and saved by Heathcliff. This incident too is milked of violence: 'Had it been dark . . . he would have tried to remedy the mistake by smashing Hareton's skull on the steps . . .' (p.97).

Juxtaposition once more: after the storm of violence comes the calm of the scene in the kitchen where Nelly is soothing her charge. It is interesting to note that the song she sings to him is a rather macabre Scots ballad about children crying and their mother listening in her grave! The long leisurely scene that follows, consisting mainly of dialogue, is important. The quiet atmosphere gradually becomes charged with emotion as Catherine compulsively talks on, and then there is the dramatic irony of the fact that she does not know that Heathcliff is present and listening (arguably a melodramatic device since it relies on coincidence). As at the start of the chapter, Nelly's placid cynicism is used to balance emotionalism: Cathy's declaration of romantic love for Edgar is deflated by Nelly's scepticism. But now Catherine becomes dominant as she strives to make clear to

Nelly how she feels about the two men in her life. The talk, essentially a soliloquy by Cathy, reaches its first climax in the heroine's assertion that she knows she was wrong to accept Edgar (p.100). There follows the description of the dream: the speech beginning 'I was only going to say . . .' (pp.101–2) is both lyrical and dramatic, using metaphor to equate 'heaven' with Edgar and his conventional love, and to equate the heath and Wuthering Heights with Heathcliff and a more powerful, unconventional love. Heartbreak and joy are marvellously evoked here.

The second climax of the monologue (pp.103–4) is in the equally powerful declaration of indestructible love for Heathcliff (now, ironically, not present to hear it) expressed in the contrasting similes of 'foliage' (Edgar) and 'eternal rocks' (Heathcliff), and culminating in the passionate assertion: 'Nelly, I *am* Heathcliff!'

After the poetic impact of this emotional climax, the crisis provoked by Heathcliff's response to what he had heard is almost anticlimax. But it is obviously of great importance in the story. The third and final section of the chapter describes the heroine's anxiety and hysteria. Then there is the atmospheric tumult of the storm, effective sympathetic background to the emotional tumult in Cathy, and to the dramatic disappearance of the hero. Finally there is Cathy's response to Heathcliff's exit – her illness. In this context, the laconic reference to the deaths of Mr and Mrs Linton, as to the previous deaths of Mrs Earnshaw and Frances, is characteristic of the author's method – it stems, perhaps, from Emily's own stoicism and reticence. Technically, the real crisis of this episode is in the actual marriage of Edgar and Catherine three years later and the heroine's fatal move to Thrushcross Grange.

bairnies Children.
grat Were crying fretfully, were vexing.
mither Mother (d.).
mools Earth, i.e. of her grave.
catechism See note p.33.
clown See note p.26.
Milo! A Greek athlete, famous for his strength, who finally tried to prise open a tree partly split by woodcutters, had his hands caught in the cleft, and was devoured by wolves.
hah isn't How is it that (he) has not? (d.)
girt eedle seeght! Great idle sight (lazy beggar).

fahl Foul (d.).

war un war Worse and worse (d.).

plottered Floundered, trampled (d.).

offald Worthless (d.).

Noah and Lot Old Testament patriarchs saved from disasters by divine intervention – Noah from the flood (see Genesis, 7 and 8), and Lot from Sodom when it was consumed with fire and brimstone (see Genesis, 19).

Jonah i.e. the bringer of the storm ('I knòw that for my sake this great tempest is upon you'. See Jonah, 1).

This visitation . . . nowt Another Shakespearean echo: 'this visitation/ Is but to whet thy almost blunted purpose.' (*Hamlet,* III,4,110–11).

lattice Probably the window itself, glass framed by cross-strips of lead, rather than a protective shutter.

starving i.e. freezing, shivering with cold (arch.).

shoo She (d.).

wer Our (d.).

Revision questions on Chapters 5–9

1 In your own words describe Catherine as a child.

2 Describe Hindley's behaviour when he became master after his father's death.

3 Give an account of the sort of relationship existing between Catherine and Heathcliff, and describe their visit to the Grange and its consequences.

4 How had her stay at the Grange changed Catherine? How did Heathcliff react to this change?

5 Give an account of Christmas day at Wuthering Heights, showing how the principal characters behave.

6 How did the death of his wife affect Hindley?

7 Why was Catherine attracted to Edgar? Briefly list the chief differences between Edgar and Heathcliff.

8 Carefully summarize Catherine's conversation with Ellen on the evening of the day she accepted Edgar's proposal. What does this reveal about her and the dilemma she faces?

9 Summarize the events of the story after Catherine finds that Heathcliff has gone.

Chapter 10

Lockwood is ill after going to Wuthering Heights, and four weeks go by before he hears the rest of Mrs Dean's tale.

Catherine and Edgar settled down at the Grange, both the Lintons doing all in their power to make Catherine contented, and the marriage became steadily happier. But Heathcliff returned unexpectedly, some six months after the wedding. He had changed greatly, being now very much a gentleman, handsome, tall, and mature, all traces of degradation vanished. He was invited into the parlour, Catherine 'too excited to show gladness'; despite himself Edgar was impressed by the change in Heathcliff. The visitor stayed a while, Catherine deliriously happy and clearly hoping that he and her husband might grow to like each other. Heathcliff then left to go to Wuthering Heights, where, it seemed, Hindley had invited him to stay!

Heathcliff visited Thrushcross Grange, soon quite regularly, and walked on the moors with Catherine and Edgar's sister Isabella. According to Joseph he spent much of his time encouraging Hindley to drink and gamble, and winning the latter's money from him at dice. It then came to light that Isabella was in love with Heathcliff, though he was uninterested in her. Catherine was incredulous when she heard, and tried to convince her sister-in-law that Heathcliff had a 'pitiless, wolfish' nature and must not be thought of as a possible husband. But Isabella was infatuated and could not be dissuaded. Catherine mockingly revealed the girl's passion to Heathcliff in Isabella's presence, embarrassing her acutely, especially as Heathcliff showed not the slightest interest, except clinical curiosity. However, Nelly felt that Heathcliff would use Isabella's love in some way in order to hurt Edgar, in revenge, just as he was harming Hindley for vengeance.

Commentary

The short break in the main narrative before Nelly resumes is interesting for two reasons. The first is the typical switch from Heathcliff's present time (visiting his sick tenant) to his past, the primary concern of the story; the second, related to the latter, is the deliberate, ironic refusal of the author to fit Heathcliff into any of the stereotyped situations of the Gothic tale of mystery (see p.111, the paragraph starting 'With all my heart!').

The next point of interest in the narrative proper is the stylistic one of the use of organic metaphors. The first of these, the figure of the thorn embraced by the honeysuckle, illustrates the essential difference between the Lintons and the Earnshaws (pp.111–12). The second is as good: Catherine's emotional instability is compared with the chemical instability of gunpowder. The third, 'sunshine' metaphor, though less original, is pleasing in its naturalness and simplicity (p.112), and tends to recur in the story, often related to Nelly Dean's own traits of homeliness and simplicity.

We are now struck by the relentless progress of the story: Catherine's 'growing happiness' is not to persist – Heathcliff returns to ignite the fuse that will detonate the gunpowder. The contrast between Catherine's passive contentment with Edgar and the violence of her happiness at seeing Heathcliff again is significant. We know that her vision of happiness is doomed, for it depends upon the naive hope that Edgar and Heathcliff will become friends. The central interest of the narrative here is the transformation of Heathcliff – the paragraph beginning 'I descended . . .' (p.115) describes it directly. Subsequent dialogue shows that essentially he is unchanged; in particular his love is unchanged. His assumption that Catherine's love for him too is unchanged, and his 'Nay, you'll not drive me off again' suggest powerfully that confrontation with Edgar, and danger for Catherine, are both inevitable.

The new phase of the story, Heathcliff back and re-established at Wuthering Heights, carries the sense of foreboding from the start. The motifs of vengeance and love merge, and the reader feels, as so often in the novel, that the former will flourish at the expense of the latter. Hindley is under Heathcliff's control, and now Isabella, fatally in love with the 'wolfish man', a 'daemon lover', gives the hero-villain another opportunity to reveal his cruelty and appetite for revenge. The reinforcement of the sense of Heathcliff's irresistibility, through the brusqueness of its description in Joseph's dialect, is also highly effective (see pp.122–3).

The onward drive of the story through the interplay of feeling and character now produces two more powerful scenes. The first is when Catherine ruthlessly exposes Isabella's infatuation (note the animal references, used to stress the idea of violence, culminating in the centipede simile (p.125) that marks the violence of Isabella's humiliation and the power of Heathcliff's hold over her). The second scene takes place after Isabella has gone out. It suggests the use to which Heathcliff will put Isabella's helpless emotion, despite his denial of all interest in her. The simple but dramatic Biblical image at the very end of the chapter evokes the potentiality for evil in Heathcliff, and sharpens the suspense (p.126).

sizar A student admitted to Cambridge at a reduced fee in return for doing certain chores. The author's father had been a sizar at St John's College, Cambridge.
earn honours . . . foster-country A reference to the war of American Independence (1775–83).
sough A drainage furrow.
beck Brook.
naughty fondling i.e. wicked or foolish girl (wicked for telling lies).
whinstone See note p.30.
crahnr's 'quest enah Coroner's inquest enough (d.).
grand 'sizes Sessions of the county court to dispense justice.
Broad road i.e. the road to destruction. cf. the title of the book, 'T' Broad Way to Destruction' (3,51).
pikes Turnpikes. The sense is, 'to make his way easy'.
justice-meeting i.e. a meeting of justices of the peace – magistrates.

Chapter 11

Passing the gate at Wuthering Heights one day, Nelly met Hareton and was shocked by the change in him: he was obviously a neglected child.

The next time Heathcliff came to Thrushcross Grange he was seen by Nelly embracing Isabella. Nelly told Catherine who angrily accused Heathcliff of making love to a woman he did not love. He admitted that revenge, not love, was his motive – revenge against Edgar, though, not Catherine. Later, Edgar tried to eject Heathcliff but was unnerved when his wife took Heathcliff's side, calling her husband a 'sucking leveret'. Heathcliff left, but Edgar had been deeply humiliated. Catherine then behaved rather hysterically, and there was another violent scene between her and Edgar in which the latter told his wife that she must choose between him and Heathcliff. Catherine had another fit of hysterical temper and locked herself in her room.

Edgar told his sister that if she encouraged Heathcliff he would disown her.

Commentary

The chapter seems to fall into three parts. First we have the meeting between Nelly and the barely-recognizable Hareton, the author typically playing with the time factor, manipulating Hindley's past, his present, and the fusion of the two times in Hareton. There is the clever juxtaposition of the meeting itself, Nelly tearful and offering love, the child, lacking mother, lacking a real father, needing love but rejecting love, consumed by suspicion and hostility, in the process of being corrupted by the devils residing in his home. This passage is pure narrative, simple and compulsive, the rapid dialogue reflecting shock, the symbolism of stone and orange natural and effective.

The pace of the story now reflects the pace and violence of Heathcliff's courtship of Isabella, one of the central concerns of the second section of the chapter. First there is the kiss, spied on by Nelly. Then comes the quarrel between hero and heroine over Isabella. Heathcliff knows he has been 'treated infernally' by Catherine, and will not be consoled by flattery but by revenge on her relatives by marriage. Love for Catherine is still the very centre of Heathcliff's life. He is not convinced when Catherine says that she will be hurt if the marriage takes place, but it is possible that if Edgar had not come in and so provoked the confrontation between the two men, Catherine might have succeeded in talking Heathcliff out of his plan, as she herself said (p.134). But Nelly now acts as catalyst, telling Edgar of his visitor's behaviour.

So the principal scene occurs (pp.131–4). This is dramatic story-telling, largely through the revelation of violent feelings in dialogue. From the first there is the irony that Catherine sides with Heathcliff, accusing her husband of listening at the keyhole, cutting viciously at him with sarcasm. There is the violent poetry of Heathcliff's sarcasm supplementing Cathy's: 'Cathy, this lamb of yours threatens like a bull! ... It is in danger of splitting its skull against my knuckles. By God! Mr Linton, I'm mortally sorry that you are not worth knocking down!' Although she knows Heathcliff might easily knock his enemy down, she precipitates violence by preventing Nelly from calling for assistance, although her sense of justice is also at work. Her act of throwing the door-key Edgar wants into the fire is perhaps melodramatic, but it does provoke the nervous collapse that is such a dramatic illustration of the essential weakness of her husband. No doubt the central device of the scene is the presentation of the violent collision of feelings and desires by means of the contrast between the main figures: Edgar, the lamb, the leveret, the mouse, the milk-blooded coward on one hand; on the other, Heathcliff, bull, king, devil. The figures of speech, stated or implicit, poetically dramatize the conflict.

This quarrel is ended by Nelly's diplomacy. Its aftermath is the concern of the third part of the chapter. It deals with the hysteria that Nelly rightly ignores as far as possible, and then with the 'ultimatum' scene, which demonstrates Edgar's conventional moral strength and Catherine's despair and intolerance of what she sees as her husband's emotional stupidity.

The chapter ends with the normal device to persuade the reader to continue: Edgar's threat to Isabella that she will be disowned if she marries Heathcliff. Perhaps such an incentive is unnecessary, for when we last saw Catherine she had blood on her lips and flashing eyes.

the farm i.e. Wuthering Heights.
warn him i.e. Hindley.
sand-pillar i.e. pillar of sandstone.
gait See note p.28.
my young lady i.e. Isabella.
lay Forget, put aside.

Chapter 12

Nelly did not worry too much about Catherine, for she thought her illness was 'an act'. On the third day she accepted some food, but was clearly ill, distraught and bewildered. Her talk became more delirious, revealing home-sickness (for Wuthering Heights) and sorrow for her lost girlhood and her lost love, Heathcliff. Alarmed, Nelly was about to summon Edgar when he came in and was shocked at his wife's condition. The doctor came (telling Nelly that Isabella and Heathcliff were about to elope) and was hopeful that Catherine would recover; the danger was permanent damage to the mind rather than death.

On a moonless winter's night Isabella ran off with Heathcliff. Edgar disowned her as sister.

Commentary

The narrative spell continues potent. First there is the tension caused by Isabella's infatuation, the rift between her and Edgar, the 'wolf' lurking near yet another fold. Then there is the isolation motif: Catherine alone in anger and illness in her room, Edgar alone with his books.

The typical balance, the parallelism we see throughout the story in the co-existence of the ordinary and the unusual, is present once more when Catherine talks to Nelly, showing hysteria, hostility to her bookish, apparently indifferent husband and a strong sense of foreboding: she talks much of death. And Catherine's face is ghastly. The suspense is sharpened by Nelly's reluctance to call Edgar, and the longer she delays the worse Catherine gets. Dramatic enlargement of the heroine's fear of death, especially death in alien surroundings, is achieved in her delirious talk as, Ophelia-like, she empties the pillow of its sad feathers (p.139). And still we have the redressed balance, in such things as the pathetic symbolism of the lapwing and the nest full of tiny skeletons on one hand, and Nelly's comment 'There's a mess!' on the other. It is in part because of this balance that the constrasting sadness and illness in Catherine evoke such pathos.

The central tension increases through the hallucinations, particularly when Catherine thinks she is back in her old childhood room at the Heights: at this point, when she says 'Oh, if I were but in my own bed in the old house ...' we are conscious of another of those moments of eerie complexity – Catherine's spirit striving to enter her old room now, Lockwood's recent past with the dream of a ghostly Cathy pleading for entry into the very same room, the merging of past and present, of death, life, and spectral existence (later to have an even more powerful part in the story). The delirious Cathy in one of her dreams is twelve years old again but wrenched from her home and converted 'at a stroke into Mrs Linton ... wife of a stranger: an exile, and outcast ...' (p.141–2). So we have the extra strangeness of this dream-child coinciding in time and space with the child-ghost of Lockwood's nightmare. At such complex moments, so many-layered that they are impossible to clarify completely, the run-of-the-mill raw material of the Gothic horror tale is transformed into poetic fiction of a high order. In the midst of her delirium Catherine utters the words that echo through the rest of the book: 'But, Heathcliff, if I dare you now, will you venture? If you do, I'll keep you. I'll not lie there by myself: they may bury me twelve feet deep, and throw the church down over me, but I won't rest till you are with me. I never will!' (p.142–3). This is dramatic, but in the context of dream and delirium and actual suffering it is not sensational, and as the climax of the scene it is brilliantly effective.

they put pigeons' . . . die A reference to rural superstitions about the indigestibility of pigeon – a common alternative to salted meat in the winter diet of country gentlemen. Catherine probably means that pigeon meat causes indigestion and therefore insomnia; by poetic extension pigeon feathers prevent death, another sort of 'sleep'.
moor-cock Red grouse.
red i.e. with the lapwings' blood.
elf-bolts Bolts (arrows) shot by fairies.
press See note on 'clothes-press', p.28.
teasing Angering, upsetting (stronger in meaning than it is today).
the oak-panelled bed See 3, p.49.
bridle-hook i.e. to which to tether a horse.
mischievous Wicked, evil (much stronger in meaning than the word is nowadays).

Chapter 13

Two months later Catherine was better, but still weak and depressed after her brain fever.

Isabella, now married to Heathcliff and living at Wuthering Heights, wrote Ellen a letter telling of her wretched life there, despised by the servants, and cruelly treated by her husband. She had something in common with Hindley, now obsessed by the desire to regain his money, win Heathcliff's, and then kill his tormentor! She asked Ellen to tell her brother that she would like to see him, but not to mention any details of her distress.

Commentary

One of the many strengths of the novel is the variation in pace accomplished without serious slackening of narrative interest. After the abduction and the crisis of Catherine's illness, the tempo drops appropriately, and through the pellucid glass of the prose we see the heroine's convalescence, Edgar's hopes, Cathy's feebleness, the coming of the bitter-sweetness of spring. The vital narrative interest of whether Catherine will live is now intensified by the news of her pregnancy — Edgar would like a son to prevent his estate going to Heathcliff via Isabella. Catherine feels she is soon to die.

The other, long section of the chapter is devoted, by means of a change of narrator, to Isabella's letter, to provide some variety of method and also to give drama and credibility to Isabella's story by means of the directness of person-to-person communication. Just before Ellen reads the letter there is another moment of authorial time-juggling: when she says of the letter, 'I keep it yet. Any relic of the dead is precious . . .', we have another fusion of times, Isabella's past revealed in an account of her wretchedness.

The letter is perhaps overlong. Its purpose is to develop the motifs of hatred and revenge by demonstrating the absence of love at Wuthering Heights. Not only does the newly-married girl have no love from her husband, but she suffers positive hatred, scorn, and physical cruelty.

brain fever We still use this imprecise term to indicate acute inflammation of the brain. It is possible that Catherine had meningitis.
gripe Clutch (arch.).
ganging Going (d.).
say See.
mud Must.
thible A stick for stirring porridge etc.
nave Fist (d.).
pale Skim (d.).
guilp Pot (d.).
deaved Broken, beaten out (d.).
meeterly clane Clean enough (d.).
mells on't Meddles with it (d.).
madling Fool, simpleton (d.).
plisky Rage (d.).
hahse i.e. the sitting-room.

Chapter 14

Edgar sent a message back to Isabella by Ellen that there could be no more contact between the two households. Ellen found the girl miserable and listless. Heathcliff confessed that they hated and despised one another, and made no secret of the fact that he had married her simply to obtain power over Edgar. It was clear too that Isabella was virtually a prisoner at Wuthering Heights.

Heathcliff obtained from Ellen an account of Catherine's illness, and said that he intended seeing her. With Ellen's help, he insisted, this could be done without the risk of another encounter with Edgar. Her instinct was to refuse, but Heathcliff said that if she did not promise to take a letter to Cathy and to help him see her, he would lock her up till the next day.

Since Heathcliff was resolved to see Cathy, Ellen saw that she would have to do what he wanted: prepare the sick woman for his visit, to take place during Edgar's next absence from home.

Commentary

Nelly resumes control of the narration, and the first interest is what is going to happen to Isabella and how she will react to Edgar's rejection of her.

Now Heathcliff dominates the dialogue as he dominates his wife, brutally crushing her with contempt and hate, calling her abusive names. His statement that 'no brutality disgusted her' (p.163) perhaps carries a sexual implication too: there is the suggestion that her husband's verbal sadism may well have been physical in the brief period of their married life, and that there is a corresponding masochism in Isabella. Certainly there is a hint of this in a woman eager to marry a man capable of hating her brother and hanging her pet dog. Heathcliff now talks like a madman, as Ellen says, hoping that he can torment Isabella into madness and so have her committed to a madhouse. We may also be reminded here of another, more famous madness – that of Rochester's wife in Charlotte Brontë's *Jane Eyre*; she too is locked up, though privately. Heathcliff and Rochester have much in common, and there is little doubt that a strong element in both is sexuality as imagined by women authors totally inexperienced in sexual matters.

The central love theme is now advanced through Heathcliff's refusal to abandon his love to Edgar's 'duty' and 'humanity'. His ferocious sincerity convinces us that life without Cathy is indeed 'death and hell' for him, and his determination to see her as soon as possible prepares us for the next critical phase in the story.

The prose, especially the prose of the dialogue when Heathcliff speaks, has intensity, fluency, and Shakespearian echoes [the brilliant 'oak in a flower-pot' analogy (p.165) is reminiscent of Hamlet's claim that his love for Ophelia is far greater than that of her brother]. Another good figure is the sea/love analogy (p.161) – again with its strong echo from *Hamlet*.

except one i.e. Catherine, 'belonging' to Isabella as sister-in-law.
brach Bitch.
magisterial Edgar was a magistrate by virtue of his social position.
dree Long, slow, wearisome.

Chapter 15

Ellen waited until the following Sunday, three days later, before giving Heathcliff's letter to Catherine. Heathcliff, who had been lurking near the house for days, came in shortly after Catherine had read his note (Edgar had gone to church). Catherine and he held each other passionately for a long time. She had a pale, unearthly look, and Heathcliff was in despair for he knew she was dying. Catherine spoke bitterly of her approaching death, and of how Heathcliff and Edgar had broken her heart. He denied this. Then she spoke more calmly, asking him to come to her, and they again embraced passionately. Heathcliff said she had betrayed her own heart and killed herself, but he forgave *his* murderer (Cathy), though not hers – Edgar. Heathcliff tried to go, but Cathy would not let him, clinging to him even when Edgar approached and came in. Cathy had fainted, and Edgar forgot his rival in his anxiety for his wife. Heathcliff told Nelly he would wait in the garden.

Commentary

The first paragraph is used for the transfer of the narration from Nelly to Lockwood, but it is a rapid transition and is only a token break in the flow of the story. The narrative interest of course focuses on the coming meeting of Heathcliff and Catherine. The paragraph beginning 'Mrs Linton sat . . .' (p.167) gives a moving picture of the heroine tragically awaiting death – pale, an 'unearthly beauty' in her face and form, dressed in white. Here, and in the two subsequent paragraphs, there is a lyrical delicacy and tranquillity in the prose that produces a good deal of pathos, and the church bells and the water music of the brook gently symbolize the permanence of Life and the impermanence of love and life for the individual.

The narrative pace speeds up with the preparation for the coming of Heathcliff, his imminent arrival dramatized with sure skill through suggestive detail: the open doors of the house, the servant out of the way, Cathy puzzling over the note, the watchdog outside suddenly wagging its tail, the step in the hall, the slight delay before the right room is found.

The love scene that follows, one of the most significant in the novel, succeeds in being very moving in its evocation of passionate emotion: the hero's perception that the woman he has loved for so long is dying; his futile despair; the bitterness, the savagery of expression that reflects the futility; the last reconciliation, the frantic kisses and caresses exchanged by people who know that they have somehow been cheated by fate and that it is all now too late. The lyrical intensity of the prose, breaking into dramatic dialogue that flows strongly, sustains the emotional tension throughout the scene and gives a sense of the reality of the emotions that dispels any suggestion of melodrama. The violence of love in Heathcliff makes him helpless to do anything but hold Catherine, who is somehow, we feel, changed back into the girl who loved him before her seduction by the false social values of Thrushcross Grange. Her refusal to let her lover go even when Edgar comes into the room is the climax of the scene and reinforces the tragic fact that she knows that she has betrayed her own heart, as Heathcliff said, and that 'it is the last time' they will ever be together in life.

Notable poetic and dramatic peaks in the scene are Heathcliff's first sentence and its accompanying description (p.169); the paragraph starting 'In her eagerness . . .' (p.171) with its powerful image of union; Heathcliff's bitter speech beginning 'You teach me now . . .' (p.171); and the simplicity of the final words in the paragraph commencing 'Damn the fool!' (p.173).

teased Handled roughly, harassed.
that glorious world i.e. some kind of spiritual afterlife, but not the
  orthodox heaven of Christian theology. There is an obvious
  connection here with Emily Brontë's mysticism.

Chapter 16

At midnight that same night Catherine gave birth to a premature daughter, and died soon afterwards. She looked beautiful in death, utterly peaceful. Ellen went out to tell Heathcliff, but somehow he already knew. In the torment of his grief he prayed that Cathy too would suffer torment, and that she would haunt him and never leave him alone in his earthly hell.

Before the burial the following Friday, Heathcliff slipped in to say goodbye to his love in her uncovered coffin. As she had wished, Catherine was interred in the open in the churchyard, (not with her own or Edgar's relatives). Her husband was the only family mourner. A simple headstone marked the grave.

Commentary

This brief chapter deals with the final phase of the Heathcliff-Catherine love relationship before the death of the heroine. Naturally the emphasis is on pathos: the puny baby, two months premature (destroying Edgar's hopes of a son), Cathy, peaceful and quite done with raging, the two sleepers in the morning sunshine – Edgar exhausted in grief, Catherine calm and lovely in death. The description is delicate and restrained, creating an image of the human condition as well as one of specific bereavement. The paragraph beginning 'Next morning . . .' (p.174) is a good example of the gentle dignity of the prose, and Ellen's thoughts in the following paragraph are surely those of Emily too, pointing beyond the myth of the Christian heaven to a more dignified if vague eternity 'where life is boundless in its duration, and love in its sympathy, and joy in its fulness' (p.175).

The bereavement motif, displacing that of vengeance for the time being, centres upon Heathcliff, leaning against a tree and accepted by the innocent ring-ousels busy with their nest (another tiny but effective symbol of the inextinguishable life of nature and perhaps also of the natural love that Catherine and Heathcliff might have had). His pride makes him defy Nelly to show him pity, but the splashes of blood on the tree are eloquent, if melodramatic. When his grief breaks through, it produces the superb monologue beginning 'May she wake in torment!' (p.177), emotion flooding and finding relief in the violence of its release. 'Be with me always,' he says to his dead love, and for once the ironic Emily, delighting in her role of God, grants his request: much of the rest of the story deals with his obsession with the dead Catherine who is also not dead in some strange but real way.

The language of Heathcliff's outburst is as extreme as the grief it describes, literally and figuratively: 'abyss', 'haunt me', 'drive me mad', 'I *cannot* live without my life! I *cannot* live without my soul!' And after this *cri de coeur* he dashes his head again against the tree and howls 'like a savage beast getting goaded to death with knives and spears' (p.177). But the aftermath is soothing, dropping into quiet understatement to balance what goes before in the monologue: the rest of the chapter is written in unemphatic prose, simple, direct, slow, and clear, affecting the reader like lyrical poetry and generating pathos without straining for it – the brief funeral, the delicacy of Heathcliff's farewell visit to his Cathy and Nelly's sense of justice in entwining and replacing the locks of hair, the grave in a corner of the kirkyard, as near the moor as makes no difference.

securing . . . son's Old Mr Linton left his estate to Edgar and his son(s), but not his daughters; if he had no son, it went to Isabella and her son(s).
ousels Small moorland birds of the thrush family, with a white crescent on their breasts.
fain Wishing.

Revision questions on Chapters 10–16

1 Describe Heathcliff's return after an absence of three years. How had he changed? In which ways was he unaltered? How did Cathy react to his return?

2 Describe (a) Cathy's reaction and (b) Heathcliff's, on hearing about Isabella's infatuation.

3 What does Ellen learn of life at Wuthering Heights from the boy Hareton?

4 Describe in detail the quarrel scene in which Edgar strikes Heathcliff.

5 Give an account of the illness Cathy suffers following this upset.

6 What did Ellen learn of (a) Isabella's marriage and (b) life at Wuthering Heights, from Isabella's letter?

7 Give a brief account of Ellen's visit to see Isabella at Wuthering Heights, showing what this reveals of Heathcliff's attitude to his wife and his attitude to Cathy and her illness.

8 Describe Heathcliff's Sunday visit to Thrushcross Grange to see Cathy. Explain what this reveals about the nature of their love for each other.

9 Describe how grief makes Heathcliff behave in the garden.

Chapter 17

After dreadful experiences at Wuthering Heights – Heathcliff had almost killed Hindley while the latter was drunk, savagely trampling on him and beating his head against the stone floor, and in another incident had thrown a knife and wounded Isabella – Heathcliff's wife escaped to Thrushcross Grange. She would dearly have liked to stay, to look after Edgar and Catherine's baby, but Heathcliff would have made her go back to him. She said her brother must not know of her visit, and left very soon to go south, near London, where a son (Linton) was born to her in a few months. She never returned, though she did correspond with Edgar. (After his wife's death Edgar became a complete recluse, though soon his daughter Cathy was the apple of his eye and a great consolation).

Six months later, Hindley died, and Heathcliff became the new owner of Wuthering Heights, because Hindley had mortgaged his property to him to pay his gambling debts. Hindley's son Hareton should have gone to his nearest relative Edgar, but Heathcliff did not permit this, saying that if Hareton were taken, he would force Isabella's son to come to him instead – thus Edgar's hands were tied.

Commentary

The death of Catherine and the atmosphere of mourning are reflected in the return of winter. There is unobtrusive symbolism here, for Catherine had loved spring, and Edgar had given her 'golden crocuses', the earliest flowers at Wuthering Heights and emblems of hope (see 13,149). Now snow comes to bury the crocuses and Catherine too – literally and metaphorically.

But life goes on: the hysterical entry of Isabella begins the episode about her life with Heathcliff, 'that incarnate goblin'. This means that there is another change of narrator, once Isabella's story gains momentum, though there is no sense of a break in narrative continuity. But the focus does shift abruptly from death and unfulfilled love to the motif of vengeance, though the grief theme is maintained by virtue of the continued presence of Heathcliff. There is sharp contrast between him as lover and mourner, on one hand, and as hater and avenger on the other. To balance the stress laid on the grief motif in the previous chapter, considerable detail is now produced via Isabella's fear, anger, and vindictiveness to stress Heathcliff's violent, non-human traits. 'I gave him my heart, (she says) and he took it and pinched it to death, and flung it back to me' (p.181). When not haunting the Grange, he is locked in his room, on the verge of 'murderous violence'. When it comes, the fight between Heathcliff and Hindley is a consummation of their mutual hatred and also a powerful illustration of the violence that permeates the story like blood pulsing endlessly through arteries and veins. The narrative and descriptive prose of this scene has a typically graphic, dramatic quality – the paragraph beginning 'The charge exploded . . .' (p.185) contains the violent crisis and is a fine example of the flowing, pictorial strength of the language. The description of the victor next morning, showing not triumph but 'eyes ... nearly quenched by sleeplessness, and weeping' (p.187), and 'lips devoid of their ferocious sneer and sealed in an expression of unspeakable sadness', marks the return to the grief motif and reminds us that Heathcliff's natural violence is aggravated almost to the point of madness by Catherine's death. Isabella is also brought into the theme of vengeance and violence: her love for Heathcliff has turned to hate (dramatically symbolized by the incident in which she strikes at her wedding ring and throws it into the fire, (p.180)). She desires Biblical vengeance: 'an eye for an eye'. She describes how she taunted her husband with Hindley's resemblance to Catherine, and roused him to murderous anger by saying that if Catherine had married him she too would have found her love turning rapidly to hate and disgust (p.189). The final picture of the violence at Wuthering Heights in this sequence is that of Hareton hanging the litter of puppies (p.189). Perhaps it should be said that there is some ambiguity about this incident, since it is possible to argue that 'litter' might refer to a basket or box containing the puppies. But this is an unlikely explanation, especially as the hanging seems to be a deliberate echo of Heathcliff's hanging of Isabella's dog (p.145), probably to suggest symbolically the corruption of Hareton through association with the evil presence of Heathcliff and Hindley. The hellish atmosphere of Wuthering Heights is thus vividly created in the detail of Isabella's picture of the 'purgatory' from which she has escaped.

Hindley's death, which ends the chapter, marks an important

moment in the theme of revenge, for Heathcliff now has Wuthering Heights, and plans to avenge himself further by corrupting his enemy's son. The garish illumination of this desire is achieved through the menacing power of organic metaphor wedded to dramatic irony: 'Now, my bonny lad, you are *mine*! And we'll see if one tree won't grow as crooked as another, with the same wind to twist it!' (p.194). At this point we can hardly share the lawyer's hope that the insatiable Heathcliff will 'deal leniently' with the natural heir to the Earnshaw property (see pp.192–3).

starve See note p.39.
stanchions i.e. the upright pillar dividing two windows (probably of stone or wood).
 basilisk A fabulous deadly reptile, also called the 'cockatrice'. The word is used more than once in the novel in reference to the evil blackness of Heathcliff's eyes.
tent Care (d.).

Chapter 18

The story omits twelve years. The second Cathy, now thirteen, was almost as much a recluse as her father, who educated her himself. Inheriting her mother's love of the moors, she longed to go to Peniston Crags – Edgar had forbidden this as it was near Wuthering Heights. However, while her father was away from home during Isabella's last illness, Cathy tricked Ellen and slipped off to the Crags; Ellen, distraught, later found her charge safe at Wuthering Heights: Hareton had met Cathy and taken her to Peniston Crags. Luckily Heathcliff was out. Cathy was disgusted to learn that Hareton, whom she had taken for a servant, was actually her cousin! Ellen told Cathy how her father hated the Heights, and made her promise not to tell Edgar that she had been there.

Commentary

After the deaths of Catherine and Hindley, the main interest of the story shifts to the new generation, Cathy, Edgar's daughter and his sole interest in life. The description of her, aged thirteen (pp.194–5), is typical of the prose style in its economy, clarity, and precision. Cathy is in many ways a combination of the best qualities of the Earnshaws and the Lintons: she is sensitive, high-spirited, attractive — but inevitably somewhat spoilt. It is clear that although she has been brought up to be almost as much a private person as Edgar, this is a suppression of her true nature and vitality, as her yearning for the symbolic 'golden rocks' of Peniston Crags suggests.

The narrative tides of the novel are never slack for long, and now they flood in strongly as the description of Cathy is left behind and the character is caught up in events she helps to bring about. Since her father is away, Cathy may play: the excursion to Peniston is the beginning of her adolescent self-assertion. Cathy's delight in her escapade, perhaps an echo of her mother's visit to Thrushcross Grange with Heathcliff, Nelly's anxiety, the girl's dismay on learning that Hareton is her cousin — all these are used to good effect in consolidating character interest and furthering the plot, though the narrative appeal is more subdued than in most previous chapters.

Hareton too emerges strongly in this chapter, and the sketch of his appearance and personality balances that of Cathy (see pp.201–2), though it is technically more interesting. This is because of the central organic metaphor, comparing Hareton to a plant struggling to grow amongst rank weeds. Hindley and Heathcliff have stunted the boy's growth, the former by taking no interest in him, the other by withholding all formal and moral education as part of his revenge on Hindley. (And Joseph has not helped by flattering the boy as 'head of the old family'.) The figure of Hareton as a 'good thing' lost in a 'wilderness of weeds' (p.201) reminds us of the equally vivid metaphor of the 'crooked tree' used by Heathcliff after Hindley's death to indicate the way he intends to influence the growth of the sapling Hareton (see p.194). Hareton is obviously an important part of the revenge motif, and Joseph is also associated with it here, for it pleases him to think that the author of Hareton's corruption, Heathcliff, will ultimately have to face God (the God of the Old Testament) and answer for this and all his other sins by submitting to divine wrath and vengeance (p.202).

Penistone Misprint for 'Peniston'. The name was no doubt suggested to Emily Brontë by a quarry quite near the parsonage called 'Penistone Quarry'.
Galloway A small horse originally bred in Galloway, Scotland.
goblin-hunter Presumably the will-o'-the-wisp or jack-o'-lantern

(phosphorescent light seen over marshy ground and caused by gas emitted by decaying vegetation and igniting).
comminations Threats of divine vengeance.
train Followers (canine).

Chapter 19

Isabella died and Edgar brought home her son Linton, a delicate, difficult child. Cathy was delighted at the idea of having a 'real' cousin to live with her, but Heathcliff sent Joseph for the boy the very night he arrived! Edgar refused to wake his nephew up for further travel but said he should go to Wuthering Heights the next day. For his dead sister's sake Edgar was distressed at having to do this, but had little choice.

Commentary

Isabella is dead; Cathy joyfully awaits the return of her father with her 'real' cousin. At once we have the thematic suggestion — the interaction of birth and death: Isabella's literal death in the background, and the approaching (spurious) love of Cathy for Linton in the foreground. Always there is the sense of duality or contrast: 'real' cousin and unreal love; 'unreal' cousin and real love for Hareton already growing, one-sidedly but inevitably.

Mild suspense is created by means of Cathy's impatience and drops with the arrival of Linton. His bad temper does not show itself at this early stage, but his exhaustion and illness do, and they activate the maternal instinct in Cathy most charmingly.

The rest of the chapter has three main linked interests. First, there is the pathos associated with Linton himself; ill, bewildered, his mother dead. Secondly, to counteract but also emphasize this pathos through contrast, there is the positiveness of Cathy's vitality and affection as she treats her cousin with suitable delicacy (p.205). Finally we have the emotional violence, contrasting with Cathy's delicacy, of Joseph's barbaric arrival and demand: he is the intrusive element, agent of Heathcliff's continuing desire for revenge on Edgar. As in other scenes of emotional violence, Joseph's dialect makes even more brutal the emotional impact of his demand. It is hard, at such moments, not to see Joseph as an agent of the Prince of Darkness, despite his Sunday clothes.

'bout Without.

Chapter 20

Early next morning, to prevent Heathcliff's arrival at the Grange, Ellen took the bewildered and fearful boy to Wuthering Heights. Linton had never heard of his father and was most reluctant to go. Ellen did her best to reassure him and prepare him in some measure for his new life, but Heathcliff received his son with a contempt that increased Linton's fear, proclaiming that he would 'endure the whelp' only because he was the prospective owner of Thrushcross Grange – he would be educated and looked after properly, though. Linton was frightened of staying at Wuthering Heights, but Ellen had to leave him, for nothing could be done.

Commentary

The emphasis of the technique throughout this chapter is on the creation of pathos out of the fact of Linton's helplessness. Uprooted again, strangely early in the morning, before he can see Cathy, he is bewildered. He is to be taken to a father never heard of until now, strangely different from his gentle uncle – bigger, sterner, with black hair and eyes. Nelly's diplomatic efforts to reassure him make sharper the ultimate contrast between her gentle lies and the violent truth about Heathcliff's personality and motives. So Linton's cry of 'I can't tell where you mean to take me' is genuinely pathetic, the appeal of a helpless victim who is not to be helped. Nelly's idyllic picture of the Heights and its environs, with its references to 'nice rambles', reading in a 'green hollow', and the 'healthier' air is manifestly false and ironic.

The culmination of this process is the image of the victim handed over to the tyrant in his stronghold; the 'low-browed lattices' and 'crooked firs' of the Heights intensify Linton's fears because of the symbolic suggestion of villainy in their ugliness (p.210). Throughout the scene of the meeting of son and father, the boy's helplessness and bewilderment are contrasted with the very unpaternal verbal savagery and decisiveness of the hero-villain.

The pathetic climax of the scene is Linton's cry 'Don't leave me! I'll not stay here!' (p.213) which touches the reader with the sense of tragedy. It may not be Heathcliff's intention to ill-treat his son physically (consumption will see to that), but we have deep misgivings about his emotional and moral welfare.

dainty Fussy.
rebuilding Presumably the sense is 'receiving' or 'encouraging'.

Chapter 21

Cathy was upset by Linton's disappearance, but time passed and her memory of him grew faint. At the Heights meanwhile Linton had a sorry life, always ill, despised by most of the household, his poor temper aggravating his problems.

On her sixteenth birthday Cathy and Ellen met Heathcliff on the moors. He invited them into the farmhouse, Ellen protesting at Cathy's acceptance of the invitation. Cathy then found out that Linton had been living just four miles away all this time – she failed to understand why relatives living so near each other did not exchange visits. It was Heathcliff's wish that the two cousins should fall in love and marry, so that there would be no dispute that they would be joint successors to both estates.

When Cathy returned home, her father forbade further visits to Wuthering Heights, telling her of Heathcliff's malevolence towards Hindley, Isabella, and himself. Weeks later Ellen discovered that Cathy had been carrying on a secret correspondence with Linton. She burnt the girl's love letters before her eyes, under the threat of showing them to her father, and stopped the correspondence forthwith.

Commentary

Omitting three years, the story once more leaps into the future, to Cathy's sixteenth birthday, also the anniversary of her mother's death so never celebrated (again, notice the interaction of the duality of life and death). The episode of Cathy going on to the moors to see the grouse nests is narrated with the customary strong, delicate touch, the atmosphere of the moorland setting captured with a sure visual imagination and reinforcing with the sense of spring our perception of the vitality and youth of the new heroine. The paragraph beginning 'I put on my bonnet . . .' (p.215) is typical of the lyrical simplicity of the style.

By one of the coincidences that are rather jarringly obvious as contrivances, Heathcliff is at the site to accuse Cathy of harassing the nesting birds, and so subtly blackmail her and Ellen into accepting the invitation to visit Wuthering Heights and thus see Linton once more. The two passages describing and contrasting Cathy and Linton (pp.217–18) are vivid and concise, preceding the chief interest of the scene; the exploitation of the inter-relationship of the three cousins to dramatize, effectively, Cathy's impulsiveness and sense of fun, the contrasting sense of inferiority and 'gaumlessness' in Hareton, and Linton's spite and snobbishness. Though illness makes Linton a sympathetic figure at first, especially when he must also be seen as a victim of the tyrant Heathcliff, his malice towards Hareton modifies our feelings. Moreover, there is a sharp contrast between the healthy potentiality of Hareton and the weak, emotionally barren Linton. Cathy is clearly more akin to the former: they are both handsome, healthy, and good-natured creatures, divided only by the artificial barriers of education and rearing, as Heathcliff was from Catherine. The essential difference between the two young men is illuminated in another formal figure of speech combining metaphor and antithesis: 'one is gold put to the use of paving-stones, and the other is tin polished to ape a service of silver' (p.221). Already Heathcliff's liking for Hareton, his perception of the moral worth of the youth, is undermining his desire for further revenge on the departed Hindley.

Back at home, forbidden to go again to the Heights, Cathy is amazed at Heathcliff's 'blackness of spirit', his remorseless and calculating acts of vengeance (p.224). What now follows, given Cathy's pride and need for self-assertion, is predictable and credible: the charming and sometimes comic episode of the clandestine correspondence. The most vivid scene in this sequence is the burning of the letters; a noteworthy technical detail is another use of the recurring image of the plundered nest (p.227). This of course dramatizes Cathy's feelings, but also takes the reader back in time, first to the delirium of Cathy's mother (12,139), then further back, via the account of the delirium, to the time when Catherine Earnshaw was as young as her daughter is now and running free and joyful on the moors. Thus we have a sense of the fusion of mother and daughter, past and present, death and life, old love and new love in that pattern of parallels and cross-references that is one of the most extraordinary qualities of *Wuthering Heights*, because in the end it has become an image of the totality and 'oneness' of life itself.

pinched in winter i.e. have to make do with less (because of the smaller yield of milk in winter time).
moor-game Red grouse.

nab Short, steep, rocky hill.

elastic as steel The writer perhaps has in mind the resilient steel of a rapier.

'gaumless' Stupid, unintelligent. Now usually spelt 'gormless'.

bathos Here the meaning seems to be 'depths'. The modern meaning is 'anticlimax'; 'a fall from the sublime to the ridiculous'; 'false pathos'.

extra-animal Outside our animal nature.

lath of a crater i.e. thin, weak creature.

a more experienced source i.e. Heathcliff.

Revision questions on Chapters 17–21

1 Describe Isabella's appearance on arriving at the Grange after her escape from Wuthering Heights. What does she tell Ellen about her life there?

2 What was Cathy Linton like as a child? What was Edgar's attitude to her?

3 Give an account of Cathy's excursion to Peniston Crags during her father's absence.

4 What was Hareton like at the age of eighteen? How had he been brought up?

5 Outline the events of the day Linton Heathcliff comes to Thrushcross Grange. What sort of person is he?

6 Give an account of the day Linton is taken to the Heights. What effect does this have on him? How is he received by his father?

7 Why is Cathy's excursion on the moors on her sixteenth birthday important in the story?

8 In your own words compose concise sketches of a) Linton and Cathy when they were about sixteen, and b) Hareton at twenty-one.

9 Write an outline of the 'love-letters' episode, showing what it reveals about a) Cathy, b) Ellen, and c) Linton.

Chapter 22

Walking with Ellen one day in late autumn, Cathy lost her hat over the wall of the park. She climbed down into the road to get it, but then had difficulty in climbing back up. While her companion was looking for the key of the door nearby, Heathcliff chanced to come along. He told Cathy that Linton was in love with her 'in earnest', and was breaking his heart because of her apparent fickleness – he was, she heard, literally dying for love of her. Heathcliff added that he was going to be away from home for the rest of the week. He hoped that Cathy would therefore call to see his son, for a visit from her would save him. Cathy did not entirely believe this, but told Ellen she would go, to tell Linton that she did care for him and that it was not her fault that she had stopped writing.

Commentary

In this chapter the focus of the narrative is on Cathy's unhappiness: her natural exuberance has been deadened by the end of her 'love affair' with her cousin; by her father's illness; and by her social isolation – unnatural to one of her age and temperament. Her tearful melancholy, different in kind from the motiveless melancholy of the heroines of Gothic romances, is aggravated by thoughts of how dreary her life will be when her father and Ellen are dead.

The account of the walk in the park stresses this sadness, which is reflected in the delicate, sombre descriptions of nature: the autumnal sky full of rain, the 'moist withered leaves', the stunted oaks blown horizontal by the wind, the last bluebell 'trembling in its earthy shelter'.

Less convincing is the meeting that now takes place when Heathcliff happens to come along: it is clearly a device to accelerate the Cathy-Linton love interest. Heathcliff scolds her for 'making love in play' and tells her of Linton's plight. The description of the lovelorn youth places him firmly in the stereotyped situation of the Romantic lover dying of unrequited love but capable of being saved by the womanly generosity of his *bien aimée*. The implausibility of this, reinforced by melodramatic stage mutters from 'the detected villain' (p.233), confirms our fear that the story has for the moment lapsed into the clichés of the Gothic romance. It is now inevitable that the tender-hearted heroine will go to her cousin the next day to say she still cares for him and 'will not change'.

Michaelmas 29 September (the Feast of St Michael).
diurnal Day-time (adj.).

starved and sackless Perished with cold and helpless.
canty See note on 'cant', p.35.
a Slough of Despond i.e. utter despair. From Bunyan's *Pilgrim's Progress,* where one of Christian's trials is to get across this slough (marsh, swamp).

Chapter 23

Next morning, Cathy, accompanied by Ellen, went to Wuthering Heights to see Linton, and it was obvious that when Heathcliff was away the boy was neglected by the rest of the household. Cathy was kind, but illness had made Linton very bad-tempered, and soon they quarrelled about the love affairs of their parents. Linton exaggerated his distress after a fall, and the soft-hearted Cathy promised to come again, despite Ellen's disapproval. Ellen was now confined to her room at the Grange for three weeks, her illness caused by sitting for so long at Wuthering Heights after she had got her feet wet. Cathy divided her day between Ellen and her father, nursing them tenderly; Ellen did not realize how she was spending her evenings.

Commentary

This chapter falls into two sections. The minor, introductory one contains the device of the 'prophetic detail', Nelly getting her feet wet, to sow a seed of subliminal speculation in the mind of the reader and so prepare for her illness – itself a device for furthering the action. In this section there is also a brief cameo of Joseph in his lair (p.235) – his refusal to attend to Linton is the link with the second section.

The bulk of this is in dialogue, and its main purpose seems to be to present a picture of the world of Linton the invalid (partly through the contrast of his personality with that of Cathy). He is neglected (note the symbolic absence of a good fire), ill, feeble, and petulant, for his personality is too weak to cope with his illness (which as described would appear to be acute pulmonary tuberculosis). Cathy's sweet nature makes her try hard to soothe and humour him, but verbal and emotional violence is inevitable, and the climax of this in the screaming fit and collapse (as Cathy and Ellen prepare to leave) leads to the reconciliation marked by the ballad-singing (p.240). Thus the emotional balance is once more restored.

Although Cathy's goodness and Linton's helplessness are overstressed in order to create pathos, it is perhaps necessary to point out that there is some genuine pathos in Linton, for we perceive that his very need to exaggerate and distort in order to gain sympathy is itself sad.

The finale of the chapter is technically deft, for Nelly's illness gives Cathy the freedom to visit Linton and so develop the action of the story.

elysium In Greek mythology the abode of the blessed after death, hence a state of perfect happiness.
starved See note p.63.
'But you've made . . . passion' Spoken by Ellen.

Chapter 24

When Ellen was again well, some three weeks later, she discovered that Cathy had been paying regular evening visits to Wuthering Heights. Sometimes, it transpired, these were happy occasions, but more often they were not, partly because of her cousin's illness and 'unhappy temper' and also because of the hostility of Hareton and Joseph. Once Linton had a frightening haemorrhage, but soon recovered. Cathy asked Ellen not to tell her father about the secret visits, but Ellen did, and Edgar forbade his daughter to go there again, though he said that he would write to his nephew to say that he might visit Thrushcross Grange if he so wished.

Commentary

The first interest of this new chapter is the comic element in the scene where Cathy is reluctant to read to the convalescent Nelly – the comedy of course dependent on the dramatic irony. This leads briskly, via Nelly's suspicions, to the 'ambush' scene in the bedroom, and thence to the story of the secret visits when Cathy confesses. One of the immediate interests of this confession is the description of Cathy's and Linton's conflicting views on the most pleasant way of passing a summer's day (see pp.244–5). Linton comes alive for us in the lyricism of the image as he rarely does in his petulance and pathos. Linton's idea of 'heaven's happiness' is dreamy tranquillity, whereas Cathy's is a kind of intoxication. The detailed description of nature, direct from the author's own delight in her moorland scenery, is vivid and fresh.

A second interesting part of Cathy's story is the account of the games she and Linton play with old bran-filled balls that used to belong to Heathcliff and Catherine – they bear the initials C. and H. The interest lies in the significance of the time factor, for once again we have a shivery sense of the fusion of past and present, the child Catherine, long gone, living again in her daughter, the child Heathcliff, also gone, alive in a way in the son he no doubt begot in a moment of hate-fired lust.

Clearly the principal interest of this part of the story is the inter-relationship of the three young people: Hareton, Cathy, and Linton. This too is a kind of miniature or echo of the enormously more powerful triangular entanglement of Catherine, Heathcliff, and Edgar – the second generation perpetuating the emotional conflict of the first.

Hareton, inspired by growing love for Cathy, tries to learn to read (anticipating the teacher-pupil love scenes of the final chapters). This is an important development since it takes us nearer to the possibility of love between Cathy and her Earnshaw cousin. This is far distant at the moment, because Hareton's 'mortified vanity', caused by Cathy's thoughtless scorn for his efforts, leads directly to his violent treatment of Linton and Cathy that gives the former a bout of haemorrhaging which frightens everyone (pp.247–8). The central clash in the main episode between Hareton and his two cousins does of course hinge chiefly on the contrast between Hareton's coarseness and inarticulate speech, and the educated speech of Cathy and Linton. Nevertheless the Earnshaw violence in Hareton is paralleled by the Heathcliff violence in Linton when rage makes him shriek to Hareton: 'Devil! devil! – I'll kill you – I'll kill you!' (p.247). And Cathy too has a moment of physical violence when she gives poor Hareton a cut with the whip (p.248), thinking he is going to attack her, whereas in fact he merely wishes to suggest, we deduce, that the quarrel and the haemorrhage were not entirely his fault.

Typically, the chapter ends crisply: prohibition of further visits to the Grange by the heroine means that Heathcliff's plans suffer a setback and may have to be changed. Thus suspense is created, for the reader must wonder how Heathcliff will react.

Michael The groom.
sarve ye eht! Serve you out, i.e. get his own back, give you what you deserve (d.).

Chapter 25

Mr Linton's health was now rapidly deteriorating, and he was eventually brought to contemplate the possibility of Cathy marrying her cousin Linton 'by a natural desire that she might retain – or at least return in a short time to – the house of her ancestors; and he considered her only prospect of doing that was by a union with his heir.' Edgar agreed to Cathy and Linton meeting about once a week for a walk or ride, under Ellen's guardianship.

Commentary

After a brief hiatus, this chapter presents us with the agonizing of the dying Edgar. His dilemma about Cathy is that the sole way of ensuring that she will retain the Thrushcross Grange estate is by agreeing to a marriage between her and Linton, heir to the property as Isabella's son. On the other hand, Linton is Heathcliff's son as well as his own nephew, and he suspects that he may turn out to be unworthy, even 'a feeble tool to his father'. He compromises by hoping that if the marriage takes place, Linton will prove to be more like himself than Heathcliff, and so be morally worthy of Cathy and a good husband to her. Edgar's monologue (p.252) shows us his two desires: for death, which will reunite him with his wife; and for his daughter's happiness.

It would, given Edgar's misgivings about Linton, obviously be fatal for Heathcliff's plans if Linton and Edgar were to meet. So the author prevents Linton going to see his uncle, by means of Heathcliff's veto (p.253), and keeps his moral and physical feebleness hidden from the dying man. Linton's letter is well written, dignified and eloquent, and reveals nothing of his faults and deficiencies; it is clear to us but not to Edgar that Heathcliff has had a hand in it.

The chapter accordingly ends with a tactical victory for the tyrant: Cathy and her cousin are to meet once a week near the Grange.

venture Endanger.
peculiar Own (adj.).

Chapter 26

The cousins' meeting took place in the late summer, near Wuthering Heights, not the Grange. Linton looked very ill but pretended he was better. It soon transpired that the reason for this was a great fear of his father – meeting Cathy was 'a task he was compelled to perform'. Ellen realized this, and also knew how ill the boy really was.

Commentary

Most of this chapter is a fairly detailed account of the first permitted meeting of the cousins since once in early childhood. Economical description and dialogue rapidly establish the physical deterioration that Linton is suffering: 'An indefinite alteration had come over his whole person and manner' (p.256). The narrative tension is produced largely by the pathetic dilemma of the youth's situation: fear of Heathcliff is forcing him to pay court to Cathy to further the tyrant's scheme of revenge, but his illness and moral weakness do not allow him to sustain this role physically or mentally. He must act as if he were healthy and affectionate, and the impossible endeavour to do this is destroying him. Cathy is neither old nor wise enough to understand his strange behaviour. She wishes to help her cousin and sustain the relationship, yet is puzzled and hurt by Linton's emotional fluctuations. A dramatic element in the situation is the skilfully evoked suggestion of Heathcliff's imminent arrival, so that Linton is in a state of constant fear.

gang See note on 'ganging', p.47.
nab See note p.61.
ongoings A compound for 'goings on'. The sense of 'our ongoings' is
   therefore 'what had happened' (at the meeting on the moor).

Chapter 27

A week later, with her father clearly sinking and Cathy attending him lovingly, another meeting took place. Linton was in a state of great anxiety; Cathy could not understand his conduct and badly wanted to return to the dying Edgar. When Heathcliff appeared, his son was almost hysterical with fear and begged Cathy to see him home. At Wuthering Heights Heathcliff locked them in and used physical violence to cow them. It had obviously been Linton's task to decoy the women to the farmhouse. Heathcliff said they would not be freed until Cathy and Linton were married. Cathy was more concerned about her dying father, and said there was no need to force her to marry her cousin, for she loved him, and was quite willing to do so. Ellen was imprisoned with Cathy the first night, and then in a room alone for four days and nights more, Hareton acting as gaoler but refusing to speak.

Commentary

The chapter falls into three parts. First comes a brief description of the dying Edgar, his decline running parallel with Linton's. The strong mutual love between father and daughter, delicately evoked, is a source of consolation to the dying man, who is also buoyed up by the hope that his nephew will look after Cathy when he is dead. Nelly suffers in this situation from her usual dilemma: as devoted servant she wishes to tell her master the whole truth about Linton, but also sees the logic of not 'disturbing his last moments'.

Secondly, there is the short passage which evokes the setting, an ironically perfect summer's day on the moors.

Thirdly, there comes the important meeting, significantly near Wuthering Heights. Narrative tension now derives from Cathy's dilemma as well as Linton's: she is on edge to go back to the Grange, but anxious to do her best for her cousin. His misery is nicely balanced by the robustness of her pity. The entry of Heathcliff marks the start of the sustained crisis of the action. His sadistic violence towards his son and the latter's helpless fear of his father eventually activate Cathy's compassion to the point at which she agrees to see Linton home. The fatal entry into Wuthering Heights follows; the decoy has performed 'tolerably well'.

We finally reach the climax, by way of dialogue that exploits Cathy's dilemma and so generates suspense: Heathcliff's ultimatum that the women will stay prisoners until the marriage takes place (p.266). The villain's words at this juncture are given particular force through the intensification of his scorn and determination, and at some moments he is in serious danger of becoming a stage villain, wholly melodramatic in his gloating savagery. But the intensity, clarity, and power of the prose are such that the scene never degenerates into melodrama: we are convinced that Cathy's quiet dignity is real and Heathcliff's villainous madness somehow credible and even understandable. At its best moments the scene has the poetic intensity of Shakespeare. When, the following morning, Cathy is taken out to be married, not unlike a condemned man being taken out to be executed, there is more than a touch of tragic inevitability in the proceedings.

at your service i.e. (contempt) for you.
cockatrice A reptile (the fabulous basilisk).
eft Newt.

Chapter 28

When Ellen was freed, she found that Heathcliff had apparently explained her and Cathy's disappearance by starting a rumour of their being trapped in a bog. From Linton she learned that he and Cathy were now married. She returned to Thrushcross Grange, to find Edgar very near death; she told him her story, omitting the more distressing details. Edgar decided to alter his will, to ensure that Cathy's fortune should be put in trust for her and not go to Heathcliff, if Linton should die. Unfortunately, this was not done: the lawyer 'had sold himself to Mr Heathcliff', and Edgar died before another could be sent for. Cathy escaped from Wuthering Heights just in time to see her father before he died.

Commentary

The sense of anticlimax following the imprisonment and the marriage is lessened somewhat owing to the stimulus of Nelly's anger with Linton, calm and complacent after the emotional storm he has weathered. The paragraph beginning 'He's in the court' (pp.271–2) is perhaps too much of a set-piece, but is interesting as compressed prose conveying much detail.

The last section is straightforward narrative, relying at times a little too heavily on sentimental detail. The death scene is no doubt overstressed in its detail about Edgar's bliss as in death he goes to Catherine and looks at Cathy with eyes 'that seemed dilating with ecstasy', but the emotions are kept within bounds by the brevity and restrained tone of the prose. Moreover, the image of blissful death is balanced by the harshness of the hasty funeral and the mundane detail about the will. Edgar's death is now the signal for the virtual destruction of the establishment of Thrushcross Grange by the agency of the corrupt lawer. This is

Heathcliff's triumph, the principal dénouement of the plot motifs of hatred and vengeance. After this resolution, it will be interesting to see how Emily Brontë maintains narrative interest.

winked Shut my eyes (both, not just one).

Revision questions on Chapters 22–28

1 Describe how Cathy's friendship with her cousin Linton is revived as a result of what she was told by Heathcliff when they met by the park wall.

2 Explain why Ellen's illness is important in the plot. What does she do when she discovers what Cathy has been up to?

3 Outline Cathy's account of her secret visits to Linton, and show how these were not always happy.

4 How are Ellen and Cathy tricked into going to Wuthering Heights? Do you think Linton's part in this affair is at all excusable?

5 What exactly is Cathy's emotional dilemma? What is Linton's dilemma?

6 Give an account of Heathcliff's behaviour at Wuthering Heights after he has tricked Cathy and Ellen into going inside.

7 What does Linton's conversation with Ellen, on the morning she is given her freedom, reveal about his personality?

Chapter 29

When Heathcliff became the new owner of Thrushcross Grange, after Edgar's death, he took Cathy with him to live at Wuthering Heights, and resolved to let the Grange. He refused to allow Ellen to have Zillah's place at the Heights, so she and Cathy were now to be separated. He told Ellen that he intended to take Catherine's portrait home, and went on to describe how he had felt the presence of Catherine haunting him through all the long years since her death. When the sexton was digging Edgar Linton's grave, Heathcliff had made him open Catherine's coffin: he 'saw her face again'.

Commentary

We are now given a picture of Heathcliff in his sombre triumph: master, not guest, at Thrushcross Grange. The descriptive paragraph beginning 'It was the same room' has the authentic quality of magic possessed by all great stories. He has come to take Cathy back to Wuthering Heights (he takes the portrait of Catherine too, soon after − 'Not because I need it, but') and rejects Ellen's plea that she be allowed to take Zillah's place at the Heights in order to be with Cathy. Ellen is to remain at the Grange for the new tenant: we are therefore approaching the point at which the story began, and the turning wheel is coming full circle.

Having thus revealed Heathcliff's 'unnatural heart' in these denials and in his contemptuous comments about Linton (pp.276–7), his creator now takes us into the heart of the chapter, which is an explicit renewal of the Catherine-Heathcliff love motif − the revenge motif is essentially finished now and its place is taken by the former as well as by the approaching love interest of Cathy and Hareton. The renewal is of course presented largely through the supernatural element that is so striking in the last phase of the book, although it has been present in various forms ever since the child-ghost dream episode in Chapter 3 (pp.54–8). Love, death, grief, and a supernatural presence are now potent motifs in Heathcliff's long monologue, one of the longest pieces of dialogue in the novel (pp.278–80). This is effective because of the intensity of the feeling it reveals and the dramatic quality of its visual detail, the central one being the image of the opened grave, the lover looking once more on the face of his dead love. This is a Gothic cliché, in theory, but the intensity of the expression of love and grief is the intensity of actual passion and of elegiac poetry, so that the situation is lifted out of its stereotyped mould and given tragic rather than melodramatic force. Heathcliff's arrangement of the coffins to ensure that he and Catherine lie close together in death is a symbol of the sad human desire for what is impossible: the permanence of love. It may be irrational of Heathcliff, but it is moving because of the human feeling that motivates it. The account of Heathcliff's obsession is a document of tormented love; the supernatural delicately and eerily present in the urgency of the emotion; the atmosphere of the cemetery; the idea of exhuming the newly-buried woman; the ghostly sigh; the 'unspeakable' consolation of his sense of Catherine's nearness.

The idea that from this moment Catherine's spirit has always been with him, near but never quite attainable, is the dominant dramatic factor in the story of Heathcliff's approach to death in the final chapters.

Chapter 30

Cathy nursed her husband as well as she could, receiving no aid from anyone at the Heights. Linton died very soon. Under the terms of his will all his and his wife's moveable property went to Heathcliff, who also claimed the Thrushcross Grange estate through his son (as well as through his wife). After Linton's death Cathy stayed in her room for two weeks, ill with strain, eventually coming down to the family sitting-room because she was so cold. Embittered by her experience and treatment, she showed only contempt for any overture of kindness, seeing this as mere hypocrisy, for in her time of need no one had offered help.

Thus ended Ellen Dean's story.

Commentary

The narration is now given to Zillah, a 'narrow-minded, selfish woman'. In a few pages we are given a concise account of Cathy's miserable life at Wuthering Heights, desperately nursing her husband without any help, and after his death isolated in her pride and bitterness, 'as chill as an icicle, and as high as a princess' – Zillah's similes are as homely and conventional as Nelly's.

The second part of the chapter is an account of Cathy's slow integration into the general life of the household, and the vague, painful beginnings of the love between her and Hareton – love that for Hareton at least germinated long before, possibly when he first met Cathy and took her to Peniston Crags, certainly when she first came to the Heights to see Linton and fired him to learn to read. The meagre love episode here (pp.285–6) is charming in its description of Hareton's efforts to please his cousin and in the pin-pointing of his fascination in the incident when he touches Cathy's hair, 'as gently as if it were a bird'. There is sentimentality, perhaps, in such details, but they are also technically acceptable as symbols of Cathy's return to life and normality, like the fire by which she warms her 'starved' body and the books Hareton gives her from the dresser.

Moreover, the growth of the love between the two cousins in the foreground of the story is paralleled by the slow decline into death of Heathcliff in the background, vague and darkly implicit in this chapter and the previous one, but soon to assume a more dramatic brilliance and to dominate the story in the last two chapters.

'thrang' Busy (d.).
train-oil Oil obtained from whale blubber.
stalled of Sickened with (d.), the equivalent of 'sick of' or 'fed up with'.
wake Stay up, keep awake (i.e. in order to nurse a sick person).
concern Nobody, insignificant person (contemptuous term).

Chapter 31

Lockwood, now almost well, goes to Wuthering Heights to tell Heathcliff that he will not be renewing his lease of the Grange beyond the twelve months originally agreed. (He is travelling to London at once.) Heathcliff, however, is out. He gives Cathy Ellen's note; she seems glad to have it but her manner in general is still listless and petulant – her mockery of Hareton's endeavour to educate himself is symptomatic of this dissatisfaction. Heathcliff appears eventually, looking thinner and restless, and Lockwood has a dreary meal with him and Hareton before leaving.

Commentary

Through Lockwood's eyes we now see into Wuthering Heights and watch what they do and say. The main interest lies in the relationship of the two young people, and this is presented through the maelstrom of feelings in which they are caught up. We see Cathy's hauteur and intolerance, Hareton's diffident advances and surly retreats, her crocodile tears and his conditioned response. In particular, Catherine's scorn at her victim's efforts to become literate trigger off first embarrassment, then anger, and finally explosive wrath as Hareton hits back with the only weapons he has, just as Catherine uses the weapons of femininity. But implicit in this game of emotional snakes-and-ladders is the romantic promise that the long-suffering Hareton will finally get his Catherine.

The final section of the chapter (pp.291–2) draws our attention to the irony of the fact that Heathcliff is becoming apathetic about revenge. We know that he is preoccupied with Catherine's spirit: this must erode hate and revenge in his mind. And there are powerful persuaders at work too in the young persons about him: Hareton reminds him more of his Catherine than of Hindley, he has always reluctantly liked the boy – he's the kind of son he should have liked to have, and he also seems to Heathcliff like a reincarnation of his own youth; Catherine is in some ways very like her mother. And both Hareton and Cathy have the eyes of his dead love.

jealous i.e. vigilant (fig.).
dinner-time i.e. noon.
Chevy Chase An old and famous English ballad.

Chapter 32

The following September, 1802, on a journey north, Lockwood turns aside to revisit Gimmerton, arrives unexpectedly at the Grange, and finds a new housekeeper there: Ellen Dean has gone to be housekeeper at Wuthering Heights. He goes there. The house is open, and through the window he sees Cathy giving Hareton a reading lesson; he overhears some of their talk – they seem to be in love. Inside, he hears from Ellen that Heathcliff has been dead some three months, and had a 'queer end' – and that Cathy and Hareton really are in love.

Commentary

The Hareton-Cathy story resumes through the idyllic teacher-pupil picture (pp.294–5): it is clear that the lovers have weathered their storms and are sailing in placid seas of delight and contentment. The juxtaposition of the harshness and aridity of Joseph's dialect and resentment of the love he witnesses, enhances through contrast the delicacy of the love motif.

When the narration is now handed over to Ellen, once more the domestic centre of a secure world, the reader is more interested in Heathcliff's 'queer end' than in the lovers, but he must curb his impatience and first hear about the rapid development of love between Cathy and Hareton. To whet our appetite for Heathcliff we are simply told that he summoned Nelly to the Heights in order that she should be company for Cathy and at the same time keep the girl as far as possible out of his sight: his preoccupation is making him increasingly solitary, for he is impatient of all society except that of the spirit of Catherine Earnshaw.

The love episode (pp.297–302) is full of charming and convincing detail: visual evocation of the 'house' setting, Catherine's remorse at having mocked Hareton's painful self-education, her laborious endeavour to break through the barrier of Hareton's injured pride with weapons that at last prove effective – pleas for forgiveness, sincere and strong affection, and considerable feminine ingenuity.

devastate the moors i.e. have a shooting holiday.
mensful Tidy, decent (d.).
wer See note p.39.
jocks Provisions, food and drink (d.). A 'jockshop' in West Riding
  dialect was a common eating-house.
he became i.e. Hareton.

Chapter 33

Hareton and Cathy had come together on Easter Monday. On the Tuesday, Cathy persuaded Hareton to uproot some of Joseph's favourite currant and gooseberry bushes in order to make room for a flower bed. Joseph, furious, pretended to give Heathcliff his notice, and the latter too was so angry with Cathy that he would have hit her. But her defiant tongue, and Hareton's intervention, entreating Heathcliff not to hurt the girl, made him desist. Also, as he later told Ellen, a sudden apathy came over him, sapping his power to act. Subsequently, Hareton defended Heathcliff, showing strong filial attachment, and Cathy knew she should not endanger this. Later still, Heathcliff admitted to Nelly that he had lost the desire for more revenge, that he sensed a strange change approaching, and wanted only to be united with the spirit that had haunted him so long.

Commentary

In this chapter the two narrative interests – Heathcliff and the two lovers – merge, briefly in Cathy's indiscretion at breakfast (pp.303–4), and then through the repercussions of the garden incident. Symbolically, the uprooting of Joseph's ancient fruit bushes and their replacement by Cathy's flowers is a useful idea to suggest love replacing fear and hate, the new order replacing the old. It also occasions the comic relief of the manservant's indignation. But more importantly, of course, it leads directly to the critical quarrel scene (pp.305–7), in which the provoked tyrant fails to chastise Cathy. This scene is important in marking the climax and conclusion of the revenge motif: Heathcliff is disarmed by seeing Catherine in Cathy's eyes, and there is the related suggestion that Heathcliff is increasingly in the power of his love for Catherine because of the consuming need to be with her. Such an obsession would displace the previous obsession with revenge by making the latter seem irrelevant, as, a little later, even breathing and the act of taking nourishment become irrelevant. The scene and its aftermath also accelerate the growth of love in the two cousins by demonstrating Hareton's love for Heathcliff and Cathy's mature acceptance of this.

The next vital scene again shows the collapse in Heathcliff of the desire for vengeance. Returning at dusk, he sees the lovers sitting close in the red light of the fire. 'They lifted their eyes together, to encounter Mr Heathcliff . . . their eyes are precisely similar, and they are those of Catherine Earnshaw.' This image supplements and reinforces the earlier one of the aborted blow (p.306), for Heathcliff is deeply affected. We are then taken at once into the duologue between him and Nelly, in which the vanishing of the desire for revenge is expressed powerfully in the 'levers and mattocks' metaphor (p.308). The ensuing account of his real life, given in terms of his supernatural experience, his unbearable sense of Catherine's nearness and inaccessibility, is poetic and moving (pp.308–10).

stale Steal (d.).
flaysome See note p.26.

Chapter 34

Heathcliff died in the early summer, after strange and unnerving behaviour, in which he looked ghastly yet seemed thrilled by a wild inner joy – the 'joyful glitter in his eyes' transformed his appearance. He planned to make a will, but could not decide how to leave his property. He gave instructions that he should be buried in the churchyard in the evening, with neither minister nor service, in a grave next to Catherine's. He died in the panelled bed – Catherine's old bed – and the doctor was unsure of the cause of death. The only real mourner at the funeral was Hareton, who grieved bitterly.

Lockwood is told that Hareton and Cathy are to be married on New Year's Day and will live at the Grange.

Before he leaves, Lockwood visits the three graves, and in the peace of the evening wonders 'how anyone could ever imagine unquiet slumbers for the sleepers in that quiet earth'.

Commentary

This last chapter is brilliantly effective in its account of the final phase of the haunting and Heathcliff's advance towards death. It is, perhaps, appropriate that the season is April and the weather 'sweet and warm', for this is traditionally the season of birth and renewal, and Catherine Earnshaw's favourite time of year. Suspense is kept high by means of the rapid flow of the narrative and a mass of detail to illustrate Heathcliff's feelings and his response to what he is seeing and experiencing.

First, there is the 'night walking', from which he returns with a 'strange, joyful glitter in his eyes' (when was Heathcliff ever seen looking *joyful* before!) and breathing 'as fast as a cat' (p.312). The paragraph starting 'He took' (p.312) is also dramatic in its suggestion that he sees Catherine's ghost in the garden; when he returns indoors he is shivering, not with weakness, 'but as a tight-stretched cord vibrates – a strong thrilling.' His involuntary starvation, referred to several times, is dramatic too, as has already been suggested, for food is meaningless, as meaningless as all things in comparison with the one reality: that he is approaching union with Catherine. Ghostly communion is strongly suggested in the paragraph beginning 'He did not quit' (p.313); in his occupation of Catherine's old room (p.314); in Nelly's Gothic speculation (p.314); and in the delicately frightening images of the paragraph beginning 'Now, I perceived' (p.315), where the ghost seems to be about two yards distant from him.

Throughout the episode the sense of the supernatural is evoked with the utmost delicacy and power, by means of a leisurely, precise description of Heathcliff's physical states. It is a subtle ghost, a subjective one that is real only to Heathcliff, but its impact on the consciousness of the reader is as solid as if the writer had conjured up an objective spectre, such is the atmosphere that its presence brings. The final image of the dead Heathcliff, his face and throat wet with rain, his hand eerily grazed by the familiar lattice of Lockwood's blood-and-ghost-tortured nightmare, a 'frightful . . . exultation' in the dead eyes, and the 'sharp white teeth' grinning, is a tremendous climax, and a feat of visualized description.

It is perhaps appropriate, since Heathcliff has always been a mysterious figure, that the doctor is not sure how the man died. The brief description of the burial is also appropriate, for it suggests Heathcliff's contempt for inessentials. But this austerity is balanced by the description of Hareton's grief (p.319) and of course by the lyricism of the famous last paragraph. The ambiguity of the contrast between the Heathcliff ghost legend and the 'quiet slumbers of the sleepers' is no doubt intentional, but perhaps the reader may feel that the tormented spirits are at last at rest, for they are at last together: Catherine Earnshaw did say with the greatest passion and clarity, 'But Heathcliff . . . they may bury me twelve feet deep, and throw the church down over me, but I won't rest till you are with me. I never will!' (12,142–3). When Heathcliff dies and is united with his Catherine, we experience a catharsis as draining as any in Shakespeare.

basin of coffee Coffee and tea were often served in basins or dishes in the eighteenth century.

Green The lawyer. See Chapter 28.

they refused . . . kirk A suicide could not be buried in consecrated ground.

chuck A term of endearment, e.g. 'my pretty one'.

grumbled Presumably he is envious of the lovers' togetherness (and it is hinted that he regrets he did not try to win Cathy).

the middle one i.e. Catherine's. The height of the turf and moss up the headstones shows how long it is since each has been laid.

Revision questions on Chapters 29–34

1 Summarize what Heathcliff tells Ellen when he comes to take Cathy back to Wuthering Heights after the death of her father.

2 Give a brief account of Cathy's life at the Heights both before and after her husband's death.

3 What changes does Lockwood find on revisiting Yorkshire in 1802?

4 Trace the growth of the love relationship between Hareton and the widowed Cathy.

5 Give an account of the 'garden incident' and its consequences.

6 Give an account of the various 'haunting' scenes and the 'strange change' that came over Heathcliff before his death.

7 Describe the death of Heathcliff and its effect on other characters.

8 Do you think the book has a happy ending? Give reasons to support your view.

Emily Brontë's art in *Wuthering Heights*
The characters

Heathcliff

I cannot live without my life! I *cannot* live without my soul!

Descriptions of Heathcliff: As a child, 4,64–5; as a boy of sixteen, 8,90–91; as a man, 10,112–15; Just before death, 34,311–17; in death, 34,318–19.

It is scarcely surprising that critics have varied greatly in their views on Heathcliff, who dominates the novel, for he is a complex character, though essentially, perhaps, the Byronic hero deriving largely from the author's reading (see 'Sources', p.17). He is seen by many critics as the personification of the Romantic 'grand passion', contrasting with relatively sexless figures such as Edgar and Lockwood. In Freudian terms, he personifies the 'Id', the dark seat of sex and psychic energy; like Charlotte's Rochester in *Jane Eyre* Heathcliff is certainly, in part, a figure of sexual fantasy. According to Lord David Cecil's view of the book (in his *Early Victorian Novelists*, Chapter 5), Heathcliff, with Catherine and Hindley, are the 'children of storm', whereas the Lintons are 'children of calm'. Again, Heathcliff has been thought to be a symbol of the non-human element in man, natural but impersonal, owing to his association with fire and storm and fertility. Other critics have given him a political interpretation, so that he is primarily the deprived child transformed into capitalist landlord, or a symbol of the working class degraded by Victorian society. Yet others, pointing to the author's own mysticism and Platonism, find Heathcliff a Platonic figure, driven by absolute passion, and severed from his other self, as Catherine is from him, finding no peace until the final attainment in the grave of spiritual union in the 'oneness' of life, and redeemed from evil by relearned love of nature.

Probably there is some truth in many of these ideas. What is certainly true is that, however complex Heathcliff may be symbolically, he succeeds as a character simply because his magnetism is awesomely credible. He may be a dream figure, devilish or fantastic, but we see him vividly through the clear magic window of the narrative imagination. Psychologically, too, he is credible: a proud, powerful man deprived of love and thus turning in anger to vengeance. Heathcliff, wrote Charlotte Brontë, 'exemplifies the effects which a life of continued injustice and hard usage may produce on a naturally perverse, vindictive and inexorable disposition' (letter to W. S. Williams, 14 August 1848). The fact that in some ways Heathcliff is an integral part of the Yorkshire setting – the hard, sardonic, fiercely independent, zenophobic, 'near' farm-owner Mrs Gaskell found in the West Riding – adds greatly to his credibility.

'The child is father of the man,' wrote Wordsworth, and the paradox applies to Heathcliff: his boyhood experiences determine to a great extent his personality when mature. His story begins hopefully as the 'poor, fatherless child' adopted by Mr Earnshaw, and in the end he is a landowner, 'rough as a sawedge, and hard as whinstone', according to Ellen Dean, and 'a genuine bad nature' in Lockwood's view (2,43). If Earnshaw had lived and controlled Hindley's resentment, nurture through sustained love might have made a different man of the foundling. But even while Earnshaw lives, his son Hindley's resentment is more potent than the father's love. Heathcliff, naturally stoical, endures Hindley's hatred, but exploits it coldly to get his own way, as when he secures the better colt (4,66–7). He endures illness too, for orphans learn stoicism early in life.

But Earnshaw's love and favour have given him hope, and when his benefactor dies he has to endure Hindley's vicious tyranny; only his strong love for Catherine makes it bearable – his happiest times are when he is with her, on the moors where he has freedom. When social ambition threatens this idyllic love, and he overhears Cathy saying that marriage with him would degrade her, Wuthering Heights becomes intolerable, and he leaves, his pride hurt, his love defeated but not destroyed – it is unaltered, unalterable. She is, for him, 'immeasurably superior ... to everybody on earth' (6,76). He reacts violently to Edgar's insult, but he knows Hindley is the real culprit, for it is he who is degrading him and separating Cathy from him. Accordingly, he dedicates himself to revenge against his oppressor.

After he has made his fortune and returns to Wuthering Heights, he is socially transformed and therefore acceptable. But his inner character is unaltered, still loving the married Catherine, still driven by revenge, a 'fierce, pitiless, wolfish man'. He declares that he wishes to do nothing to hurt Catherine, but ironically his behaviour leads to her death because of the destructive tension set up in her by his return and her realization that in marrying Edgar she has committed spiritual suicide. Destructive energy, not directed at the person whose perfidy has broken his heart, is directed, in revenge, along other channels. Heathcliff marries Isabella purely to obtain power over Edgar (the latter's estate will pass to Heathcliff, if Catherine has no sons, through his wife); he clearly cares nothing for Isabella's feelings, as later he cares nothing for his son, and treats her with devilish sadism (see Chapters 13 and 14, 162–4).

Reunited briefly with Catherine just before her death, his unconsummated passion for her, and the knowledge that she is dying, produce bitter anguish. It is too late for him to help her; she broke his heart by betraying her own and marrying Edgar; what might have been can now never be. All the bitterness of this is in their last embrace (15,171), and Heathcliff's speech beginning 'You teach me . . .' (15,171–2) goes to the centre of the tragic irony of their situation. Heathcliff is still holding the unconscious Cathy when Edgar comes in: 'it is the last time' and he has refused to leave her.

After her death he is demented with grief, as the scene in the garden shows (16,177); its culmination is in the plea beginning 'Be with me always . . .' (177) and in his actions: he 'dashed his head against the knotted trunk; . . . and howled, like a savage beast . . . goaded to death with knives and spears.' The plea is answered, for Catherine's spirit keeps him company in the 'abyss', haunting him through the years that follow, killing him by 'fractions and hairbreadths' (see 29,280).

He lives on, tormented by his sense of Catherine's spiritual presence, nourishing himself on the bitter food of revenge and avarice. Soon he has the satisfaction of seeing Hindley die (see 17,193–4), and looks forward to further vengeance through his plan to corrupt Hindley's son Hareton. Similarly, he terrorizes his sick son Linton, in order to marry him to Cathy Linton and so acquire Thrushcross Grange – the ultimate revenge. Heathcliff regards his son as his 'property', a 'cobweb' he might 'annihilate with a pinch'; 'his life is not worth a farthing, and I won't spend a farthing on him' (30,282). Once he and young Cathy are married, Heathcliff loses interest in them, for now both the Grange and Wuthering Heights are his.

Heathcliff also treats the child-widow Cathy savagely, keeping her a virtual prisoner, depriving her of books and company, as he has deprived Hareton of education and guidance. But Cathy and Hareton, in love, stand up to him: after the incident of the uprooting of the fruit bushes, their love, and, more potently, the ghost of Catherine looking at him through their eyes, 'thwart' Heathcliff's punitive violence: he has finally lost all desire for revenge (see 33,306–10). Thereafter, he wants only solitude, to commune with his inexorable ghost. At this point he ceases to be evil: he feels neither hate nor the desire for revenge, and the obsession is becoming so intense that ordinary life is becoming meaningless. His energy too is ebbing: 'O God! It is a long fight, I wish it were over!' (33,310).

Just before his death Heathcliff enters a state of unearthly joy: 'very much excited, and wild and glad!' He has a 'strange, joyful glitter' in his eyes'. It is perhaps the first time since his boyhood that he has felt happiness. He tells Ellen, 'I'm too happy; and yet not happy enough. My soul's bliss kills my body, but does not satisfy itself.' He walks on the moors at night and is obsessed by the terror and joy of his sense of Catherine's nearness. He has 'to remind' himself to breathe, and forgets to eat, though Ellen does her best to remind him. Finally, the intensity of the spiritual obsession brings death, for the physical life has become irrelevant. He dies, significantly in Catherine's old bed, exultation on the 'sarcastic, savage face', and the doctor is unable to find the cause of death. He is buried as near Catherine as possible, 'as he had wished' (see 29,278 and 34,319).

Catherine Earnshaw

Nelly, I *am* Heathcliff!

Descriptions of Catherine: As a child, 5,68–9; at fourteen, 7,77; after her brain-fever, 15,167; in death, 16,174–5.

After Heathcliff, Catherine Earnshaw is the most important figure in the novel, the heart of which is of course her relationship with Heathcliff. Emily Brontë gives most of her characters strong emotions, even weak figures like Linton, and Catherine's most distinctive trait is her capacity for intense feeling. She is impulsive, physically attractive, humorous, courageous, and has a vitality as powerful and natural as the wind and the moors she loves.

We first meet her as a girl in the diary Lockwood finds at Wuthering Heights, about to 'have a scamper on the moors' (for which she is beaten by her brother). Time leaps forward then, for in Lockwood's dream she reappears, as Cathy *Linton* (3,54), the child-ghost who pleads to the dreamer for admission but is, ironically, unresponsive later to Heathcliff's passionate pleading (3,57–8).

Through Nelly's story we see Catherine's personality and actions more clearly. She rapidly becomes very 'thick' with the newcomer Heathcliff, feeling a powerful affinity with him. As a child she is active, wayward, tomboyish, a 'wild, hatless little savage' running barefoot on the moors and able to ride any horse in the stable (hence her request for a whip). In her early teens, a 'wild wicked slip', she is still impetuous, pretty, and playful, an outdoor girl, a natural leader, often maddening but good at heart and 'much too fond of Heathcliff. The greatest punishment . . . for her was to keep her separate from him.' Her father's death is a severe blow, but it brings her and Heathcliff even closer, in mutual consolation.

Under Hindley's tyrannical regime 'the unfriended creatures' are well-nigh inseparable because of the need for a common defence against the oppressor. In the Thrushcross Grange escapade Cathy shows her mischievous nature, spying on and scaring the Lintons; also her courage, when attacked by the bull-dog: 'She did not yell out – no! she would have scorned to do it'; she urges Heathcliff to run and save himself.

Seduced by the upper-class culture of the Grange, the heroine returns to her home greatly changed, at least superficially, by 'fine clothes and flattery'. She is dignified and lady-like, 'quite a beauty'. From now on, though still loving Heathcliff, she is attracted to Linton, both for his own sake and because of the alluring world he stands for. The two men and their worlds are opposites, irreconcilable; unable to choose between them, Catherine develops a 'double character', conforming when with the Lintons to their social and moral values, but behaving more naturally with Heathcliff. In the presence of both, her dilemma is obvious, for she wishes to please both and offend neither – an impossible task. Consequently, she tries to keep them separate whenever possible. The stress of this dilemma aggravates the natural violence of her temper and at one point almost loses her Edgar (8,93–5), but the quarrel merely 'effected a closer intimacy' and they 'confess themselves lovers'. Social ambition, coupled with the desire to be independent and get away from

Hindley, makes Catherine agree to marry Edgar. But in her talk with Nelly (9,98–104) it is clear that she is bewildered by her position, loving Heathcliff but regarding marriage to him as out of the question as it would degrade her, because of what Hindley has made of him. The irony is that by choosing a marriage that will not degrade her socially, she violates her strong, instinctive love for Heathcliff, 'betrays her own heart' and suffers a deeper, spiritual degradation. In this conversation with Nelly she strives to be rational, differentiating between her feelings for the two men in her life, and knowing that she has 'no more business to marry Edgar Linton than ... to be in heaven'. But she is defeated by her difficulties and by the pressure upon her to make a 'good marriage'. This deepening of her dilemma is one of the dramatic centres of the story.

When Catherine falls ill she is a difficult patient, 'wearisome and headstrong', and in convalescence 'saucier and more passionate, and haughtier than ever'. The doctor has said she should not be 'crossed', and she knows this and exploits it to try and get her own way, as when Edgar tells her she must choose between him and Heathcliff (11,135–6). After this, emotional exhaustion, lack of food, and hysteria merge to produce the illness that eventually kills her. In one sense her illness is the only way she can resolve the unresolvable – the problems that derive from her desire to have the best of both worlds, Heathcliff and Edgar, the natural and the social. Her lack of realism is Catherine's undoing: 'our fiery Catherine' has in the end 'become a child' (another explanation for Lockwood's childghost?). She has in effect separated body and soul, giving her body to Edgar, and her soul to Heathcliff: death is the result of this violation.

After her death Catherine lives on, idealized, in Edgar's memory; in her daughter, who is a milder version of herself; and of course in her spiritual effect on Heathcliff. In his grief he commands her to haunt him (16,177) and she does this.

Clearly, like Heathcliff, Catherine is important in the symbolism of the novel. Through her the author explores aspects of romantic love: affinity, passion, torment, inaccessibility, spiritual fusion in death; the conflict between natural and conventional behaviour. Catherine also reflects her creator's mysticism and Platonism; her words reveal this, notably in the dream of heaven (9,101–2); the 'foliage and rocks' similes; and the central declaration 'I *am* Heathcliff', these last two in the same episode (p.103). The story of the lovers operates on the human level primarily, but it is unreasonable to deny that it is probably also allegorical, a symbol of the 'oneness' of all life that was the dominant idea in Emily Brontë's mystical vision of life. So the tragic love theme is an image of the human condition, of the vanity of human wishes, of the ultimate futility of life as the author seems finally to have seen it. But it is also symbolic of an effort to explore a deeper, spiritual reality.

Edgar Linton

Kind, and trustful, and honourable.

Description of Edgar: 7,81; 8,89 and 92–3.

As we have seen above, Catherine has two men in her life. Heathcliff's strength appeals to the depths of her nature, but Edgar is weaker and so attracts her less powerfully, more superficially, appealing to her head rather than her heart. Edgar is a social being, wealthy, respectable, morally conventional, educated, and Catherine's social self responds to this, not with passion but with admiration and worldly desires. Heathcliff is malevolent and strong; Edgar is benevolent and weak – 'he lacked spirit in general'. There is physical contrast too: Edgar is fair, slight, conventionally good-looking, with delicate features and a gentle voice – a typical Linton. Much of the imagery used to describe him illustrates these attributes: 'honeysuckle', 'a beautiful, fertile valley', 'lamb', summer 'foliage', 'moonbeam', and so on.

From the start Edgar is strongly attracted by Catherine's vivacious beauty: when she is taken into the Grange in the 'spying' scene (6,76) he 'stood gaping at a distance'. But he talks well, and when he visits Wuthering Heights at Christmas he is sarcastic about Heathcliff's hair (as his nephew Linton is later about Hareton's accent and illiteracy) – and later lies about it. He becomes aware that Catherine's vitality and impulsiveness can produce violent ill-temper (8,93–5), but love sweeps away his misgivings, and he is very happy when they marry, three years after his father's death and Heathcliff's disappearance. If the latter had not returned, the 'deep and growing happiness' of the marriage might have given them both lasting contentment. But Heathcliff's catalytic impact is violent: Catherine is delirious with joy (an emotion Edgar is unable to arouse in her) and Edgar accepts Heathcliff for her sake. But of course the stress of coping with the situation leads eventually to breakdown – both in the marriage and in Catherine. Edgar thus shows weakness in hoping for the best, but we sympathize with him in his dilemma. We sympathize too in the quarrel scene, when the 'lamb' threatens like a bull but collapses when Catherine sides with his enemy (11,132–4). His negative personality is also shown when he allows the distraught Catherine to remain in isolation while he consoles himself with books, though he is consumed with self-reproach when he finds how ill his wife is.

He does not forgive Isabella for marrying Heathcliff: his brotherly love and moral sense are perhaps both feeble in this instance. But it is understandable that potential goodness in Edgar is incapable of becoming active because of the constant threat posed by Heathcliff. We see this aborted goodness clearly when Edgar brings Linton home but is unable to keep him: his gentleness and sorrow contrast with the hero-villain's moral violence (see Chapters 19–20).

After his wife's death, Edgar becomes a recluse, and the death wish is morbidly strong in him. More positively, though, he dotes on his daughter, devoting himself to her welfare, but he is overprotective and to some extent lives vicariously through Cathy. He is wise, we feel, to forbid her to visit Wuthering Heights, and it is ironic that he is deceived into thinking that Linton may have integrity and be good for Cathy. His hopes cannot be fulfilled, for his enemy's vindictive energy is irresistible. But the irony of events also compensates him posthumously: his procrastination over the will costs his daughter the inheritance, but later gives her a more suitable husband in Hareton and restores the inheritance after Heathcliff's death.

Hindley Earnshaw

He had room in his heart only for two idols – his wife and himself.

Descriptions: newly married, 6,71; in final dissipation, 13,152.

Hindley is a key character in the motif of revenge and violence. We first meet him briefly in the flashback in Chapter 3, newly married but acting tyrannically towards Heathcliff and Catherine. Thus he is already associated with the theme of revenge before we know why he exacts vengeance. When he reappears in Ellen's narrative as a boy of fourteen, all is made clear. His father has brought home the 'cuckoo' and Hindley is resentful, first childishly on account of the smashed fiddle and because the foundling is so obviously a 'foreigner', and later because he regards the newcomer as an usurper. His aggressiveness, which seems innate, is thus aggravated when his father's protective attitude towards the orphan turns into favouritism. He abuses Heathcliff verbally and physically, on one occasion endangering his life (4,66–7). His hatred causes so much friction that his father sends him away to college. When, after old Earnshaw's death, he becomes master at Wuthering Heights, he reorganizes the household to suit himself and his wife, degrades his adopted brother by depriving him of education and reducing him to servant status, and treats his sister badly too. After the Grange escapade, he is determined to separate Cathy and Heathcliff, and his actions become increasingly violent and vindictive.

Had his wife lived, domesticity might have redeemed Hindley. But when she dies, soon after his son is born, he goes to pieces: 'When his ship struck, the captain abandoned his post; and the crew, instead of trying to save her, rushed into riot and confusion, leaving no hope for their luckless vessel' (17,191). Grief for Frances, whom he had adored, now turns to despair, to hate of both God and his fellow-men, and soon to dissipation, drinking and gambling with 'bad companions'. His drunken tyranny is unbearable (see 9,95–8) and almost results in Hareton's death – the child is terrified of his father, and when Ellen has to leave to go to the Grange with Catherine, on her marriage, the prospects for the five-year-old boy are frightful. Wuthering Heights is now infamous, and Ellen tells Hindley that 'he got rid of all decent people only to run to ruin a little faster'.

Hindley's final phase of degeneracy starts when Heathcliff comes back and lodges with him. All Earnshaw's bitterness and hatred now focus on him, and when Heathcliff's avenging exploitation of his old enemy's weaknesses takes effect, the hatred becomes homicidal (see Isabella's letter, Chapters 13 and 17,182–9).

Eventually, Hindley loses all his money to Heathcliff, who becomes the mortgagee of Wuthering Heights, and the luckless man's sole interest in life is to win his money back, get Heathcliff's too, and then to kill his persecutor. This forlorn hope is not fulfilled, and Hindley dies in a drunken fit about six months after his sister's death. Only Ellen grieves for him, and Wuthering Heights passes to Heathcliff.

Cathy Linton

She's a beauty, it is true; but not an angel.

Descriptions: At the age of twelve, 18,195; at sixteen, 21,215, 218; as a young widow, aged seventeen, 2,42; at nineteen, 32,295; compared with Hareton, 33,307–8.

We meet Cathy early in the novel in Lockwood's narrative (Chapter 2) – handsome, withdrawn, hostile. She reappears as Catherine's premature baby, born just before her mother dies, a 'moaning doll of a child', at first unwelcomed but soon wielding 'a despot's sceptre' in her father's heart. So when Catherine Earnshaw departs physically from the story, her place is taken by the second heroine, 'the most winning thing that ever brought sunshine into a desolate house'. At the age of thirteen she has her mother's impulsiveness and vitality, but the Earnshaw wildness is toned down by the Linton meekness. She is perhaps by nature an outdoor girl like Catherine, but because her father is a recluse she is a captive spirit: she has no friends, rarely goes outside the park, and is somewhat spoilt by the doting Edgar, anxious to educate and protect her. She compensates for lack of freedom by constant mental activity, and sometimes shows resentment in tears and petulance.

The independence and freedom for which she increasingly yearns are symbolized for her by the 'golden rocks' of Peniston Crags. Taking advantage of Edgar's absence when Isabella dies, the 'cunning little fox' eludes Ellen and escapes. Her subsequent meeting with Hareton, the excursion to the Crags, and the visit to Wuthering Heights all mark her emergence into the world and, ironically, the beginning of her long and sterile association with Linton and Heathcliff.

When Cathy meets the pathetic Linton (Chapter 19), she shows what a warm and sociable nature she possesses: she is 'wild with joy' at the prospect of having a companion, and treats her cousin with delicacy and sweetness. His disappearance is a blow she does not get over for many weeks. The resumption of the friendship when she is sixteen is at first delightful to her, and she is astonished to learn that he has been living so near to her for three years. But once more the friendship is severed when her father forbids her to go to Wuthering Heights because of Heathcliff's evil nature – a fact of life Cathy learns now for the first time. She is a spirited girl, and so the ensuing 'love-letter' episode is quite plausible; it seems a delightful and romantic contrivance to her, and it reflects her sweetness and adolescent simplicity. The burning of the letters is a great sadness for her, and the end of 'her little romance' naturally makes her life duller and sadder. There is true pathos in the shock and disappointment she suffers.

The phase that follows (see Chapters 22 and 23) shows Cathy being emotionally blackmailed by Heathcliff into seeing his son, and this is credible because of the vulnerable warmth and compassion of the heroine. Certainly the fluctuation of her emotions in the secret meetings that take place during Ellen's illness is entirely plausible (see 24, 243–50), for it is triggered by the interaction in her of sympathy and frustration, both of which are realistic responses to Linton's personality and behaviour.

The scenes that show us the dying Edgar (27,258–9, and 28,273–5) reveal Cathy's devotion to her father, and it is this factor that gives credibility to the forced marriage that follows the decoy and imprisonment episode. The marriage, preceded by the kidnapping, inevitably has a melodramatic quality, which does perhaps lessen the reader's interest in Cathy as an individualized character. Nevertheless, the basic story remains believable because it depends on the credibility of the villain: Heathcliff's magnetism and the 'diabolical violence' of his aims and actions have such strange vitality that we accept him as readily as we accept the potent figures in dreams. Consequently, we see Cathy's actions as a bowing to the inevitable. She is sincere in saying that as she loves Linton there is no need to force her into the marriage, for she would gladly accept her cousin without compulsion. Her submission is made more plausible by Heathcliff's terrible violence to her (27,263), and also by our belief that her falling into the emotional trap Heathcliff set for her is made credible by her compassion and inexperience – Hareton and Linton are the only young men she knows and it is quite possible that she should think that what she feels for Linton is love.

After the sadness of her father's death and the distress caused her by Linton's, Cathy has the resilience to survive. She shows her mother's pride and anger in her contempt for the people who did not help her when she most needed help in her husband's final illness, but gradually emerges from isolation and begins to live once more, aided by Hareton's warmth and interest.

The account of the last phase in Cathy's story (from Chapter 30 on) shows, quite credibly, the triumph of love over hate, of youth over sad experience. At the beginning of the phase she is 'as chill as an icicle', and 'as high as a princess'; at the end the 'smiling beauty' of her face reveals the happiness she has won with Hareton. Once the educational difference between the lovers lessens, it is clear that Cathy and her cousin have enough in common to make their future hopeful: they are physically well-matched and share the Earnshaw temperament. Their love is in part a thematic device to restore the 'old order', to re-establish stability after the chaos caused by Heathcliff, to 'join the two houses' in a manner reminiscent of Shakespearean dénouements.

But it is surely true that the love story of the final chapters is feasible in its own right, in spite of its moments of sentimentality and overstatement. At certain points it merges with the 'haunting' motif, gaining poetic intensity by the association, as when Heathcliff returns at dusk and sees the lovers together in the firelight.

Hareton Earnshaw

Gold put to the use of paving-stones.

Descriptions of Hareton: At eighteen, 18,201–2; as a young man, 2,42–3.

As with some of the other characters, we first meet Hareton through Lockwood's narrative (see Chapters 2 and 3), 'rude' in dress and speech, but with a 'free, almost haughty bearing', and reacting to Cathy's derision with Heathcliffian savagery. But in the main chronological narrative he begins life as a 'fine boy' born to the dying Frances; Ellen maternally compensates, but he is still destined to be the deprived child, terrified soon of his father's 'wild beast's fondness or his madman's rage'. When Heathcliff comes back to Wuthering Heights after his long absence, Hareton begins to look upon him as his real father, for Hindley is unnaturally intolerant of the boy, whereas Heathcliff once saved his life and now says he 'mun do as he will', and he also to some extent protects Hareton from his father's drunken violence. We know that the hero-villain has an ulterior motive in thus being a surrogate father, but this is naturally not known to the boy: he develops a strong attachment for Heathcliff that never weakens.

When Ellen sees 'her child' (11,127–8), he is already 'lost': emotionally deprived, neglected by and hating his father, spoilt by Joseph, and looking up to Heathcliff because he 'pays dad back what he gies to me – he curses daddy for cursing me' and because he prevents the curate coming to educate him. It is hardly surprising that Hareton feels grateful to Heathcliff, and that with no gentle, motherly influence but with a 'devil daddy', he models his behaviour on that of Heathcliff. When Nelly comes to offer him love and oranges, he gives her in return hate and suspicion, and throws a stone at her (accurately!).

We next see Hareton as the 'ruffianly child' of Isabella's letter (13,151–2). He is 'strong in limb and dirty in garb, with a look of Catherine in his eyes and about his mouth'; he swears at her and threatens to set the dog on her; his boorish aggression is a direct product of his environment – Wuthering Heights under the grim control of the two devils Heathcliff and Hindley. Heathcliff has made him 'scorn everything extra-animal as silly and weak', and the boy's action in 'hanging a litter of puppies from a chair-back' is a double symbol – of Hareton's corrupted innocence and of the hellishness of the house in which he lives.

When his father dies, Hareton is completely dependent on Heathcliff, who does not maltreat him physically, partly because of the lad's 'fearless nature', but his intention is clear: to make his 'bonny lad' grow as crooked as Hindley, 'with the same wind to twist the tree'. Hareton's prospects are bleak, but 'the unsuspecting thing' does not know this. He is subsequently brought up as a 'clown', isolated, uneducated, without wages, ignorant of the injustice he suffers.

Ellen sees evidence in him at eighteen of a mind 'owning better qualities than his father ever possessed', a 'healthy soil that might yield luxuriant crops under other and favourable circumstances'. Hareton is angered by Cathy's assumption that he is a servant and not a 'real cousin', but he soon forgives her and tries, inarticulately, to make his peace with her (18,201). He is naturally rather intolerant of Linton, and jealous too, for his affection for Cathy is growing and Linton is a rival. He rightly resents the latter's snobbish malice and Cathy's thoughtless mockery of his efforts to improve himself, relieving his hurt pride with violence (24,247). But again he is sorry, and tries to explain his attitude and to make it up with Cathy. Similarly, his generous spirit is evident when he is the only one to pity and offer aid to the dying Linton. Unlike Heathcliff, he is truly a rough diamond, and after his cousin's death he shows kindness in wishing to help Cathy; from this moment their love grows, slowly and erratically because of the ups and downs caused by Cathy's mockery and his reactive violence, but it does grow. And when Cathy finally realizes the folly of her behaviour and the 'gold' in Hareton's nature, his resentment is quickly extinguished in the delight of his realization that she is sorry and wants his friendship and love. Cathy's love socializes and at last civilizes him: 'He had been content with daily labour and rough animal enjoyments till Catherine crossed his path.' Now, in the sunlight of Cathy's love, the rank weeds wilt and the plant grows tall, strong and fruitful.

Linton Heathcliff

The worst-tempered bit of a sickly slip that ever struggled into its teens.

Descriptions of Linton: As a boy of twelve, 19,204 (compared with Edgar); at sixteen, 21,217–18.

Linton's obvious traits are physical frailty, self-pity, ill-temper, and cowardice. When he first arrives at the Grange (Chapter 19) his pallor, thinness, and cough suggest the inevitable 'consumption', possibly caught from his mother, who has just died of it. Because of his condition and background, the imminence of his move to Wuthering Heights, and the brutality of Joseph's arrival (19,206–7), we are at first genuinely sorry for Linton, for he is perfectly credible. But in the ensuing five years, controlled by the puppet-master Heathcliff, he becomes less so and the pathetic quality in him is so excessive, so obviously needed for the sake of the plot, that it rings somewhat hollow.

It is arguable that Linton, child of a mismarriage, inherits the worst qualities of his parents. At any rate, his delicacy, fairness, and slender physique, as well as his educational and social background, are typical of the Lintons. From Heathcliff he perhaps gets his violent temper, his selfishness, and the malicious tongue that ridicules Hareton's illiteracy (21,221–22). His self-centred nature expresses itself also in self-pity, which, coupled with lack of spiritual stamina, makes it impossible for him to fight his illness or show Heathcliff any defiance.

Removed at once from the Grange, where he would have had love and sympathy, Linton is doomed from the start. At Wuthering Heights later, socially groomed for marriage with his cousin but growing up there 'in utter lack of sympathy', his illness worsens and the 'unhappy temper' accompanying it is aggravated. A 'peevish creature', a 'whey-faced, whining wretch', he seems to have no future at a time when ordinary, healthy folk have their whole lives to look forward to. So we do feel sorry for him; this is also why Cathy's strong compassion is credible.

Cathy does her best, when she visits him, for she is a sweet-natured girl, but his ingratitude, petulance, and selfishness are hard to cope with. When he is fairly well, early in the friendship, his malicious, snobbish attitude towards poor Hareton rather alienates us, as it disgusts Ellen and Heathcliff (and perhaps even Cathy when she reflects upon it). The episode of the 'love-letters' reveals sweetness in Cathy; in Linton it reveals a sour selfishness that suggests that he may be incapable of love and is certainly not worthy of Cathy's: 'You should have come, instead of writing. It tired me dreadfully, writing those long letters' (23,235). When they play games, they quarrel, as he is a bad loser. They have some pleasant moments, but most of the time Linton makes Cathy unhappy, bewildered, and frustrated, not knowing how to please the sick, bad-tempered boy, who takes his companion's good nature for granted. The truth is that quite apart from his illness Linton and Cathy are unsuited to each other: she has the Earnshaw vitality and warmth; he has the Linton passiveness and coldness. The passage contrasting their views on the pleasantest way of spending a summer's day, illustrates this incompatibility: Linton's motif is tranquillity, but Cathy's is intoxication (24,244–5).

The final scene on the moor, when his terror of Heathcliff gives him a 'coward's eloquence' and makes him 'manage tolerably' as a decoy, shows him at the lowest point of his degradation – an agent of evil and utterly in his father's power. An even baser moment, not at all easily credible, is the scene after the marriage (28,270–2) when Ellen, just given her freedom, finds him 'sucking a stick of sugar candy' – this symbol of immaturity perhaps makes him for a moment a sympathetic figure. But his long complaining speech beginning 'He's in the court . . .' (p.271) reveals selfishness, spite, lack of imagination, lack of love for his child-wife, and even pleasure at the sight of his father violently punishing her. His conscience may trouble him a little, but he has now lost the reader's sympathy. He is, as Ellen says, 'a wretched creature . . . with no power to sympathize with his cousin's mental torture.'

This is his last direct appearance. His death, quite feasibly occurring soon, gives Cathy back the freedom she should never have lost, though it also gives the tyrant Heathcliff the revenge he has worked for: triumph over the Lintons and possession of Thrushcross Grange.

Isabella Linton

My heart returned to Thrushcross Grange in twenty-four hours after I left it.

Descriptions of Isabella: At eighteen, 10,117, 119–20, 125; as Heathcliff's wife, 17,179–80.

Isabella has much in common with her brother, for they are both products of their class. She is conscious of her breeding and social status, appropriately dignified (until she meets Heathcliff), and, in general, temperamentally passive. Everyone likes her, with her yellow hair, delicate indoor complexion, and 'dainty elegance'. Just as Edgar is physically inferior to Heathcliff, so she is inferior to Catherine, physically and in personality. Living a socially unnatural life, for her class and wealth entitle her to a wider range of contacts, she wants a husband to gain independence and the conventionally desirable status of a married lady – it is ironic that she makes a most unconventional match. She is clearly infatuated with Heathcliff: he is only incidentally a means of escape to freedom (another irony). She resents the general disapproval of her love for the hero-villain, which merely strengthens the feeling. Catherine is furious with her, tries in vain to talk the girl out of her infatuation, and finally exposes Isabella's 'secret' to Heathcliff maliciously, in her sister-in-law's presence, and so causing her deep embarrassment (10,123–5). Ellen also warns Isabella, telling her of the true Heathcliff and his way of life (10,122–3), but passion blinds

Isabella, who feels that the whole household is against her, though there is probably some truth in her claim that Catherine is a dog in the manger. So Isabella mopes 'about the park and garden, always silent, and almost always in tears', until Heathcliff courts her rapidly, ruthlessly, having decided to avenge himself further on Edgar by marrying her. She hopes for the best, but Heathcliff's sadistic act of hanging Isabella's pet spaniel before the girl's very eyes, the night they elope, is an evil omen. Heathcliff has no heart of gold. He treats her, as he said he would (10,125), in a 'very ghoulish fashion', with physical and emotional savagery. The two months the married couple spend away from the region must have been terrible for Isabella. At Wuthering Heights her life is hideous, love and marriage both turned to bitter desolation (see 13,150–58, and 17,179–90). Heathcliff makes no secret of the fact that he would like to drive her mad and then commit her to a madhouse. This could indeed have happened, if Isabella had not escaped from Wuthering Heights and then gone to live near London. Her final bitterness is that she will not see her brother again, and that the child she gains from her devil's parody of a marriage is, by her own admission, a 'peevish creature' and perhaps affords her little consolation. Isabella dies of consumption, about thirteen years after Catherine's death, and through her and her son, the tyrant gains Thrushcross Grange.

Joseph

The wearisomest self-righteous Pharisee that ever ransacked a Bible to rake the promises to himself and fling the curses on his neighbours.

Brief descriptions of Joseph: 1,36; 5,68.

Joseph plays no part in the main plot, but he has several functions. First, because of his religious bigotry, he contributes to the 'tyranny' motif, notably when he is shown dominating the dying Mr Earnshaw by 'sermonizing' and making the lives of the children wretched in a similar way (5,68, and 3,50–51). He is also associated with the 'revenge' theme; Hindley and Heathcliff yearn for personal revenge, but Joseph's vengeance is his God's. He pays lip service to Christianity, but his God is the vindictive, tribal deity of the Old Testament, demanding an eye for an eye, and his lack of Christian humility is made clear: 'All warks togither for gooid to them as is chozzen, and piked out fro' th' rubbidge!' he says. He is arrogant, earthy, zenophobic, sanctimonious, but curiously able to reconcile these attributes with the conviction that he is one of the chosen. His characteristic holier-than-thou attitude goes hand in hand with a savagely unsympathetic nature – his attitude to the newly-married Isabella (see Chapter 13), and his sneering contempt for Linton (20,210, 212, and 23,235) and Cathy (2,45–6) reveal this.

Hypocrisy is almost personified in him, for his practice does not reflect his preaching: he does not love his neighbour but hates him. He is devoid of humanity, intolerant of joy, laughter, and love. His sour face and croaking voice suit his personality, as does the crudity of his language. One of the clearest images of his unchristian malevolence is the scene where he comes to take poor Linton, like an executioner come for the condemned man (19,206–7).

However, he is not all bad: he is like Nelly, a loyal family servant. He knows who is the rightful heir to Wuthering Heights, and does not condone Heathcliff's actions: he regards him with awe, as if he were literally an agent of the devil. And, according to Nelly, he is no liar.

Joseph often gives the impression (as Ellen sometimes does) that he is a cynical, one-man Greek chorus, with a most unorthodox accent of course, a dash of Caliban, and a generous measure of the 'devil-porter' in *Macbeth* (notably in Isabella's letter episode in Chapter 13). He is probably the most interesting of the minor characters, because he is an individual, not a mere caricature of a bigoted, Yorkshire, Bible-obsessed servant.

The narrators

One of the obvious aspects of the novel is the device of multiple narration. The principal narrator is Ellen Dean, the secondary one Mr Lockwood – one a native, the other a 'foreigner', notice. But the story is also told by several other characters, most of whom are, like Ellen, important in the plot. Among these, Isabella is probably the most important, the source of much graphic detail about Hindley, Heathcliff, and her own period at Wuthering Heights (13,150–58, and 17,179–189). Heathcliff himself narrates the Thrushcross Grange adventure (6,73–6), tells us of his frantic attempt to exhume Catherine's body the night of her funeral (29,279), and so on. Zillah tells of Linton's life at the Heights and of Cathy's behaviour after his death. Cathy gives us the story of her secret visits to Linton. And there are others. In fact, there are so many narrators that we are never quite sure who is speaking, for the narrative style seldom varies enough to allow us to differentiate between characters.

Ellen Dean

I went about my household duties, convinced that the Grange had but one sensible soul in its walls, and that lodged in my body.

Ellen Dean first comes into the story as Lockwood's dignified housekeeper at Thrushcross Grange, 'a matronly lady, taken as a fixture along with the house'. At his request, she tells her employer Heathcliff's 'history'. In this she reappears as the child Nelly, 'always at Wuthering Heights', part playmate, part servant. Like the other children, she rejects the 'gypsy brat' initially, but soon 'softens' towards him. Under Hindley, she is relegated to the back-kitchen, but is a staunch ally of the 'unfriended creatures', Catherine and Heathcliff – confidante, adviser, consoler. Her conscience makes her offer help to the adopted son, though little comes of it. When Frances dies, Ellen is only too pleased to take charge of Hareton. Despite Hindley's dissipation, she loyally stays on in 'the infernal house', acting as safety-valve as well as nanny and cook, and fearlessly condemning him as 'worse than a heathen' when his drunken irresponsibility nearly gets the infant Hareton killed. She advises Catherine not to marry Edgar, by implication through her common sense and cynicism, though the misguided heroine does not take this advice, partly of course owing to the vanishing of Edgar's rival (see 9,98–110). In Catherine's consequent illness Ellen is a devoted nurse.

A family servant of Ellen's standing is naturally often faced with the dilemmas caused by divided loyalties: when Catherine marries, Ellen is glad to go with her to the Grange, but much upset to have to abandon 'her' Hareton – ironically just when she has started teaching him to read. She respects her new master for his integrity; she humours the imperious Catherine; she warns Isabella against Heathcliff. Sentimental about her old playmate, and as so often troubled in her conscience, she wishes to help poor, drunken Hindley, but fear of Heathcliff prevents her. She regards it as a moral duty to keep an eye on the prowling of the 'evil beast', and catches him kissing Isabella, though nobody can prevent the inevitable elopement. At one point in Catherine's brain fever, Ellen mistakes serious illness for hysteria, and is upset about her mistake and Edgar's criticism of her 'heartlessness' – this is another illustration of the dilemma of the 'faithful servant' (see Chapter 12), as is her tactical silence when she should perhaps have told the master about his sister's elopement.

Probably the most dramatic instance of the operation of the dilemma of the trusted servant with divided loyalties, is when Ellen is persuaded to help Heathcliff visit the dying Catherine: this seems to her a lesser evil than the alternative of another confrontation between husband and lover. The dilemma is perhaps symbolized in Ellen's sense of justice, of objective judgement, when she twists together the two locks of hair and puts them back in Catherine's locket (16,177–8).

An important new period in Ellen's life begins with her role of surrogate mother to the baby, immediately after Catherine's death. Vicarious motherhood is always close to Nelly's heart, and, as she tells us, the 'twelve years ... following that dismal period were the happiest of [her] life'. She is a primary source of Cathy's happiness as a child, and her vigilant guardian when she begins her life outside the boundaries of the Grange park. Her action in reading and burning Cathy's love-letters seems surprising, but once more it is the dilemma at work: she decides that what she does is morally defensible as it is for Cathy's own good in the long term – she clearly takes no pleasure in the intrusion. Similarly, her sense of duty makes her tell Edgar about Cathy's secret visits to Linton. When the cousins are later permitted to meet, Linton's behaviour is such that Nelly 'hardly knew what to hide, and what to reveal'. And when she is imprisoned in Zillah's room, Ellen, understandably exhausted, has a crisis of conscience that arises from her chronic state of clashing loyalties: she ascribes all her employers' misfortunes to her 'many derelictions of duty'. This is not so, but it has a nucleus of truth.

After Edgar's death, Nelly's maternal loyalty makes her plead for Zillah's place at Wuthering Heights, so that she can be with her young mistress in her time of great need (Cathy is shown to be virtually friendless in the subsequent crisis of her mismarriage to a dying man). When love grows between Hareton and

Cathy, she is overjoyed: 'They both appeared in a measure my children: I had long been proud of one; and now, I was sure, the other would be a source of equal satisfaction.' She looks forward to 'the crown of all my wishes', their marriage.

In the final phase of Heathcliff's life, Nelly does her best for him, loyalty and compassion merging, though she is often at a loss and sometimes terrified by the haunted man's face and behaviour. It is both typical of her, and symbolic of her functions, that she tries to keep his fires going and to make him eat.

To sum up: it is clear that Ellen is not simply the chief medium for the story, but also of considerable importance in the plot, and interesting in her own right. She plays a vital part in the motif of ordinariness and domestic routine – the 'canty dame' with red cheeks, common-sense, and conventional morality; she helps therefore to balance the opposed motif of high passions, ghosts, and wildly unconventional behaviour, making these more credible by her association with them. Like Joseph, she is pure Yorkshire, an organic part of the setting, though her speech is not dialect but implausibly precise if necessary for sustained narration. Again like Joseph, she is a loyal family servant, but unlike him is amiable. She is amazingly versatile: housekeeper, cook, nurse, foster-mother, confidante, companion, messenger, adviser. She has no life of her own, no apparent desire for husband and children: her life is almost entirely vicarious, lived in and for 'her' family, Earnshaws or Lintons. On the whole, Ellen does perhaps represent normal humanity, though in some measure she acts as 'chorus', much more obviously than Joseph, standing outside as well as participating in the events she describes, and so functioning, though not at all infallibly, as interpreter, commentator, judge. And because of her interaction with all the other characters, she is clearly a force for narrative cohesion.

Mr Lockwood

My home is not here. I'm of the busy world, and to its arms I must return.

Unlike Ellen, Lockwood plays no part in the main plot: he meets some of the key figures, but his contact with them is of minor interest and essentially a source of appetizing interest in them for the reader. In the first three chapters we meet Heathcliff,

Hareton, Joseph, Zillah and the unhappy Cathy through him, and glimpse the past in his nightmares. Lockwood is thus fascinated to learn more about Heathcliff, and his housekeeper duly obliges (Chapter 4); his illness gives Nelly a captive audience. She finishes her story in one week, and then Lockwood goes on with the narration. He reappears in person towards the end of the novel (Chapter 31), going to Wuthering Heights to tell his landlord that he will not renew the lease on Thrushcross Grange, and reproves Cathy for mocking Hareton's effort to become literate. In the autumn of 1802 he goes for the last time to Wuthering Heights, learning the manner of Heathcliff's death from Ellen and enviously witnessing Hareton's and Cathy's love, of which he has also been told by his old housekeeper. It is Lockwood who brings the novel to a close when he visits the graves of the three most important people in Ellen's story, and responds to the occasion with appropriately elegiac feeling.

Critics have reacted variously to Lockwood, as to Heathcliff and to Nelly: he is seen as a normal Victorian gentleman, an agreeable but shallow young man, a sketchy attempt to portray a sophisticated townee, and so on. A majority verdict, perhaps, is that he is a well-meaning but rather confused and superficial young man 'whose experiences ... provide him with an utterly unexpected education in the realities of passion' (Margaret Drabble). He is occasionally naive but he also shows signs of maturity and intelligence, in spite of many moments of foppish conceit. He is socially gauche, temperamentally passive, and perhaps without any capacity for passion. His stay in the West Riding convinces him that London is the place for him, not the former – 'a perfect misanthropist's heaven'. Like Nelly, his ordinariness (urban, not rural) contributes to the credibility of the events he is caught up in and hears of, and his interaction with the principal narrator is skilfully exploited all through the novel, in various ways, to enrich the texture of the narrative.

Structure and style

Structure

The basic episodic framework of the close-packed story is clear. The first three chapters form a leisurely introduction, giving us Lockwood, the secondary narrator, the central character Heathcliff, and Cathy, Hareton, Joseph and Zillah who reappear later in the story. After our glimpse of the past in Catherine's diary in Chapter 3, we return to the present. The real start of the story is in Chapter 4, when Ellen Dean, the most important narrator, relates to her master Lockwood the early history of Heathcliff and the Earnshaws. Here, of course, we travel back into the past again, but it is a journey that is to continue, with brief interruptions, throughout the novel, so in our imagination Ellen's memories become our present and that of the characters. At the end of Chapter 7 there is a short break in the narration, Ellen then being persuaded to go on with the 'cuckoo's history'.

At the juncture of Chapters 9 and 10 past again becomes present: Ellen goes to bed; Lockwood has been ill for four weeks. The story then continues, with the beginning of Catherine's marriage and the return of Heathcliff: we are back again in the living past. In Chapter 13 Isabella's letter – narrative within narrative – describes incidents Ellen could not have seen for herself. Ellen resumes control in the next chapter, but at its end there is another break when Lockwood sees the doctor. At the start of Chapter 15 Lockwood takes over the narration, having by then heard all his housekeeper's story – he promises to use Ellen's words, as she is 'a very fair narrator'. The story goes on to the end of Chapter 30 in which Zillah has told us of Cathy's miserable life at Wuthering Heights; at the start of the next chapter we are back where we were in the first three chapters, in Heathcliff's farmhouse with its gloomy inmates. In Chapter 32 Lockwood goes to Wuthering Heights, and Ellen concludes the story by tellling him and us (in that and the following two chapters) about how Heathcliff died, and about young Cathy's second and more promising love affair, with Hareton.

It is clear, then, that the structure of the novel involves narrative counterpointed against narrative, the past interacting with the present, in a complexity that is dreamlike and yet realistic. The central narrative thrust is so strong that it assimilates these complexities and ensures that the story is told and made memorable with impressive clarity.

We know that Emily Brontë was a mystic, and it is possible that the idea of the 'oneness' of life which was at the heart of her mysticism, and is one of the underlying themes of the novel, also effects the construction of the book. For the central structural feature of *Wuthering Heights* is its 'oneness' or unity, from which flows a powerful sense of interrelationships, cross-references, and cohesion. So the structural pattern of the book may be thought of as a sort of microcosmic image of life as the author saw it. This overall impression of cohesion and unity depends on the blending of the various different elements of the book, in particular, perhaps, in the blending of the ordinary and the fantastic. Professor Daiches said that one of the great achievements of the novel is 'the domiciling of the monstrous in the ordinary rhythms of life and work' (Introduction to *Wuthering Heights* Penguin edition), and this is surely so. Throughout the story we have this structural duality of the ordinary and the extraordinary, the latter made more credible by the presence of the former. This basic duality, a source of constructional strength and symmetry, does much to make an artistic unity of the book. And from it there flow other dualities in the shape of opposites, contrasts, parallelisms.

One of the most important of these parallelisms is the homely setting of the story on one hand and, on the other, the manifestations of violent or fantastic behaviour: passionate feelings, evil deeds, ghosts and so on. Another duality is that of the two houses, Wuthering Heights and Thrushcross Grange, literally very different and also opposing symbols of the primitive and the sophisticated, the life of the farm and the affluent life of the landowner – the poles of storm and calm the critic Lord David Cecil sees as the central idea in the book (*Early Victorian Novelists,* Chapter 5). The natural and the supernatural are another pair of opposites, and they are often brilliantly integrated, as in the final episode of the story when Heathcliff sees his dead Catherine in everything, especially in the eyes of Cathy and Hareton, which are 'those of Catherine Earnshaw'. And, obviously, there is the duality of the ordinary narrators and the extraordinary events they describe.

A similar duality appears in the characters. We have the 'children of storm' (Catherine, Heathcliff, Hindley), and the 'children of calm' (Edgar, Isabella, Frances). In the former we have the traits of strength and violent passions; in the latter, emotional weakness and submissiveness. The end of the story comes with the reconciliation of opposites: the union of the offspring of the two marriages, a blend of Earnshaw and Linton.

Other dualities that help to give strength and balance to the structure are good and evil, love and hate, births and deaths, revenge and counter-revenge. There are, too, numerous parallelisms in situations: Heathcliff's degradation is echoed in Hareton's; both products of hate and revenge, for example.

Another important aspect of the construction is the precision of the time-scheme, which aids both cohesion and credibility. It is possible to work out the dates of every important event. The very first words of the novel are a date: '1801', and from then on throughout the action, happenings are carefully timed: 'Easter Monday'; 'one October evening', for example. The passage of time is noted: 'Seven days glided away'. Sometimes seasonal references are used instead of implied or obvious dates: the golden crocuses and the primroses of spring, autumnal mists, the blizzard at the bleak start of the story, and the benign image of late summer tranquillity that marks its concluding paragraph. These seasonal allusions also contribute to the cyclical pattern of the narrative.

The saga nature of the plot produces additional structuring: events are spread over three generations and a period of some fifty years, the second half of the eighteenth century. The emphasis is, in the main, on the second generation, though the third also plays a major role in the story; the older Earnshaws and Lintons are of minor importance, except for Heathcliff's benefactor. This saga pattern is skilfully woven, so that the sense of the passage of time is always clear and we are given a strong sense of continuity (an important element in the microcosmic image of life the book presents – see pp.96–7).

Also of structural importance is the interweaving of past, present, and future. This is used continually to integrate the generations, as when Heathcliff sees his own youth in Hareton, or in the sense of the reincarnation of Catherine in her daughter. It is also a powerful source of the supernatural motif, as when Cathy and Linton play with their parents' old toys

(24,245), or when Heathcliff sees the spirit of Catherine in the eyes of the lovers (33,308). One of the most impressive of these moments of time-manipulation and supernatural impression is in Chapter 29: Catherine has been dead for eighteen years, her daughter is that age too; then Heathcliff tells us what he did 'yesterday' – taking advantage of Edgar's burial preparations to exhume his beloved's body – and then goes back eighteen years to the other attempt at exhumation the very night Catherine died (see pp.278–80). The tragic pathos of this episode lies in the image of the transience of joy and life evoked by the fusion of past and present. A similar time-fusion occurs when, in 1801, Lockwood reads Catherine's old diary, meeting her in her past youth as he has just met her daughter in her present youth; the ghost in his nightmare personifies the life of the past refusing to be extinguished, and eerily cross-relates to a later moment in the story (12,139–43) when the delirious heroine, exiled at the Grange, imagines she is a twelve-year-old girl 'wrenched from the Heights' and yearning to get back into her old room – she is shut out as the child-ghost is shut out by Lockwood (and the ghost has the right name: Linton). And of course Lockwood has seen the names scratched on the window-sill – names which stress the cyclical structure of the novel and summarize its most important events (see *Commentary*, Chapter 3, and text, p.49).

Another point to be made about the structure is the effect upon it of the author's poetic gift. The lyrical impulse in Emily Brontë helps to produce the appropriate form in *Wuthering Heights* – personal, original, and given unity as much by the flow of feeling as by the dualities, the precise time structure, and the dove-tailing of event and character. The real action of the novel is the sequence of moments of passionate emotion: Hindley's hatred, Heathcliff's despair and Catherine's terror and love in their last meeting, Heathcliff's grief in the garden, his torment and ecstasy as he approaches death and union with Catherine. Such moments of high feeling are irradiated with an intense poetic light that gives them great clarity.

Around these stark, dramatic rocks of emotion the general flow of the narrative pulses continually; there are few lapses in interest because all the time, as in real life, things are happening – births, deaths, marriages, illness, meals, walks, the life of nature, household and farm work. There are very few references to life outside the 'Wuthering Heights Triangle', however:

politics, economic developments, town life, society. This is one of the reasons why such an intensity is achieved — at times it is almost claustrophobic. There is no narrative irrelevance in the shape of sub-plots: all events relate clearly to themes, plot, atmosphere, or characters. An instinctive faculty for selection is at work, so that a kind of narrative 'survival of the fittest' operates: only those elements essential to the effective telling of the story are retained.

The novel has sometimes been attacked on the grounds that the device of multiple narration is clumsy, producing confusion and fragmentation. No doubt there is some truth in this point, but the narrators are useful in several ways. As we have noted, their use facilitates the manipulation of the time factor and of the two chief generations. Again, the device helps to maintain suspense: when Nelly stops talking to go to bed, or Lockwood muses about life, the action is suspended and we are impatient to get on with the story. Moreover, Nelly's vagueness on some points and Lockwood's mistakes and misjudgements make them more human and so aid general 'suspension of disbelief'. The whole first-person narration, though confusing at times since we are not sure who is speaking, is an aid to credibility, for the narrator — Nelly, Lockwood, Isabella, Zillah — is often both eye-witness and participant and so dependable as a source of information. Now and then there is a jarring note, as in Isabella's letter in Chapter 13, but there, as elsewhere, the power of the narrative impulse compensates for this (the letter also provides information Nelly herself could not have possessed).

An obvious merit of *Wuthering Heights* is its freedom from authorial intrusion. Emily Brontë does not intervene to analyse, moralize, or pontificate, and there are no vast set-piece descriptions. Thus the story-line is always clear to the reader; narrative credibility is also aided for we are not constantly reminded of the existence of the puppet-master.

The considerable time-spread of the novel has already been mentioned. In contrast with this element of the structure, the sense of place, as implied above, is deliberately limited: the story evolves at the two houses and on the surrounding moorland (see 'Setting and influences', pp.20–21). Gimmerton is sometimes mentioned, but it is unimportant in the plot. Because the structure of the action confines it to this area, the sense of place and of the concentration of the action is very strong, sharpening the impact of event or emotion: think of the dying Catherine spiritually shut in at the Grange, or Heathcliff on the moors, as omnipresent to his unlucky son as if he were an evil deity.

Various other structural points should be noticed, such as the use of the first and final sentences of chapters to maintain narrative tension, as when Nelly refers to Heathcliff's vindictiveness (4,67), or to Isabella's death and its repercussions (19,203) – instances are numerous. The variation in the pace of the narrative is also noteworthy: at moments of high feeling or dramatic incident, such as the last meeting of Heathcliff and Catherine, or Hindley's drunkenness and its consequence for the infant Hareton (9,95–7), the flow is rapid. At other, more tranquil moments, like the picture of the happy lovers near the end of the book (34,320–1), the tempo is suitably slower. Such variation in the speed of the narrative, like the occasional alternation of long and short chapters, is incidentally a source of variety refreshing for the reader.

Naturally enough, the novel's construction has imperfections. The artistry of the dialogue (see 'Style') is flawed with lapses into the melodramatic, such as the muttered asides of the villain. Nelly's vocabulary and style are no doubt implausible, as is the continuity of her narrative manner when Lockwood takes over the narration. Structurally more important, there are many instances of improbability or coincidence: Heathcliff overhearing Catherine's conversation with Nelly and leaving unnoticed by the heroine at the exact moment the plot requires this (9,98–102), or the meeting of villain and victim by the park wall (22,232–4). Edgar's 'blissful' death is not readily credible. There is a strong suggestion of contrivance in the use of Linton as victim and decoy: indeed, the whole of the episode concerned with the decoying and imprisonment of Cathy and Nelly and the forced marriage, is not easy to believe, despite the enormous incentive to do so provided by the personality of Heathcliff. Similarly the death of the first heroine halfway through the story sounds like a guarantee of anti-climax. But, as we have seen, (*The Characters*, pp.82–3) there is a strong case for arguing that Catherine's physical death intensifies the narrative interest in the latter part of the novel because of Heathcliff's spiritual obsession with her. Also, the rather conventional love-story of Cathy and Hareton, and the 'happy ending', are not mere additions to please the reader: they are present in embryonic form at the beginning of the story, and the second and third generations have been integrated all through the book. Cathy is a reincarnation of her mother's personality; Hareton is both an Earnshaw and also a sort of re-creation of Heathcliff's youth, his spiritual 'son', as well as being so like Catherine that the haunted Heathcliff 'can hardly bear to see him'. So, in one important sense, the redeemed Hareton (saved from degradation by his love for Cathy) leads to redemption for Heathcliff, who sheds his satanic nature when he cannot avenge himself further on the lovers. He sheds even the need for food and fire as he approaches death and union with the ghost who has kept him company in her own way for so long. The union of the young lovers symbolizes the union of Wuthering Heights and Thrushcross Grange, the old order and the new. So the third generation is structurally important in the conclusion of the plot, for their love brings calm after the storm, tranquillity after the cosmic disturbances created by passionate love, by hate and vengeance and other unnatural, destructive feelings. It is not unlike Scotland after the death of Macbeth, the restoration of goodness and sanity after the chaos of 'fair is foul, and foul is fair' – except that Macbeth goes defiantly to his doom, whereas Heathcliff, desiring at last only love, goes exultant into his death. His 'sarcastic, savage face' is finally deceptive, for his spirit is elsewhere.

Style

A writer's style is the way in which he uses language. This sounds simple, but style is complex, many qualities combining to form the distinctive manner of each individual author. Some of these qualities are essential and used almost instinctively: precision, clarity, humour, fluency, even metaphor. Others are 'detachable', more obvious devices with specific purposes, like analogy, simile, paradox, personification, or antithesis. Some literary devices, of course, are normally used in poetry, rarely in prose – rhyme and metre are obvious examples.

On the whole, Emily Brontë was an instinctive writer, using words directly as they came to her through her poetic or narrative imagination, and disdaining decorative tricks. This does not of course mean that she wrote carelessly: her art no doubt conceals much of the hard work she must have put into the novel. But she does seem to have had the gift to write rapidly, accurately, and forcefully. Her purpose in *Wuthering Heights* is to tell her strange story as clearly and credibly as she knows how. The tale is in the 'Gothic' tradition, but she avoids most of the worst stylistic excesses of the genre: endless repetition, crude fantasy, gross sensationalism, mystification for its own sake, prolixity in description, over-emotional tone, and ornate devices.

Because of this dominant purpose to tell the story directly and compellingly, the prose of *Wuthering Heights* is natural and straightforward, the style of an intelligent young woman unconventionally educated but a natural, impulsive, lyrical writer. There is no straining to impress the reader and no 'poetic' embellishment. It is vigorous and fluent, giving that sense of spontaneity that is so vital in maintaining freshness. The lyrical power of her prose gives it its flavour of originality: we feel that Emily Brontë alone could have written this story, in such a casual, matter-of-fact style. The overall effect perhaps is the quality of clarity: the window-pane of her prose is so transparent that it is as if there were no pane and we were looking into vivid illusion as if it were reality, like a dreamer accepting the reality of his dream.

The variation in the pace of the prose has already been mentioned in connection with the narrative structure (see p.107). The tempo quickens at moments of passionate feeling or exciting incident, and slows appropriately when the story is less concerned with strong emotions. Examples have already been mentioned, but it must be noted that a more rapid pace of prose is achieved in general by the use of short paragraphs, staccato sentences, considerable dialogue, fluent and forceful, often a conspicuous simplicity in the vocabulary, generous stressing, broken sentence structure, and appropriate imagery. The more relaxed, leisurely prose tempo is produced normally by the use of a less urgent tone, and by the omission of many of the devices mentioned above in relation to the quicker movement of the prose; its imagery too is appropriate: in the slow final paragraph of the novel the metaphor of sleep is used – in the rapid flow of the prose in the dramatic last meeting of the lovers, for instance, the simile of 'a mad dog' is employed to suggest Heathcliff's passion and sense of urgency (15,171).

The sentence structure, another aspect of the prose style, is also well adapted to the narrative need for immediate intelligibility and a steady flow of ideas. There are few long, complex

sentences making the meaning hard to grasp. The sentences
are usually short, and the skilful control of balance and punc-
tuation almost invariably creates a logical sequence of ideas,
clarity, harmony, and euphony. Examples are of course
innumerable, but as good as any are the paragraphs describing
the arrival of the 'gypsy brat' at Wuthering Heights (4,64–5),
the 'idyllic' description of Linton's 'idea of heaven's happiness'
(24,244–5), or the account of Nelly's discovery of Heathcliff's
corpse (34,318–18).

The vocabulary of the novel is wide in range, giving the
prose conciseness, variety, and precision. Perhaps the author's
poetic faculty is the source of this instinctive, sensitive selection
of the appropriate words. A great deal of the vocabulary
reflects a balance of Anglo-Saxon words and Latinisms, but at
times there is an imbalance: excessive use of 'bookish' terms of
classical derivation strikes a note of pedantry or awkwardness.
But this is quite rare, and found more in the prose of the
dialogue than in the basic narrative or descriptive language.
Moreover, there are very few classical allusions, and this in the
Victorian era is refreshing. One noteworthy aspect of the
vocabulary is the choice of verbs and nouns; this is unpre-
tentious generally, but many of these words clearly relate to
theme, character, or atmosphere, and so help to sharpen the
effect of the prose. For example, nouns like 'devil', 'wolf',
'reprobate', 'brute', or 'madman' stress the story's passions and
conflicts; and verbs like 'writhe', 'grind', 'tear', 'strike', or 'recoil'
reflect the violence of the action.

Normally, then, the vocabulary is simple, concrete, fresh and
direct, with only occasional use of abstract terms. There is an
agreeable absence of clichés, though these are sometimes
deployed in the dialogue or when obviously suited to the narrator's status – thus we have Nelly referring to Cathy as her
'lamb' or saying that the children were 'as quiet as mice'.

The rhythm of the prose, an important quality, is also controlled by Emily Brontë's lyrical art: as a poet she knows
instinctively how to manage the flow of the words that imagination brings to her pen. The basic rhythm of the prose, not of
course the rigidly patterned rhythm of poetry, is a continual
pulse of verbal energy, an incessant restlessness and onward
motion, like the irresistible motion of waves and the thrust and
blustering of tide or storm wind. It is an essentially natural

rhythm, produced partly by the strong direct flow of the sentence structure and the variation in the pace of the narrative, as we have just seen, and also by the skilful use of repetition, emphasis, pauses, exclamations, and rhetorical questions. There are innumerable examples of the typical prose rhythm, but the following are some of the best: the ghost sequence (3,54–5); Heathcliff's speech beginning 'You suppose' (14,161); Catherine's delirium (12,139); the lovers' final tragic meeting (15,170–3); and Heathcliff's grief (16,177). As with the pace of the narrative, the rhythm varies in intensity and onward thrust in relation to the variation in feeling and sense.

Humour is often a pleasing aspect of style, but in *Wuthering Heights* it would seem incongruous, and certainly there is little real humour in the novel. Now and then we have some amusing irony, as when Lockwood is socially awkward (2,41–2, and 43–4), and we often get touches of humour from Nelly, Catherine, and Zillah. Heathcliff's talk often contains humour too, but it is black humour, sarcasm suited to his black moods and meant to wound his victim. Similarly, there is the earthy humour of Joseph, especially savage when he is mocking Isabella (13,152, and 155–8). These moments of humour sometimes lighten the dominant atmosphere of doom and oppression, but they do not amount to very much: humour can hardly be said to be a feature of the prose style. Emily Brontë's vision is the mystical, tragic vision of Blake and the later Romantics, not the comic vision of Dickens, Thackeray, or Peacock.

'Tone' in style is that 'tone of voice' that suggests the mood of the writer – happy, ironic, enthusiastic, sad, and so on. The amazing thing about the tone of the narrative prose of this novel is that it is so casual, as if the author regarded her story as a perfectly ordinary one. As has been said before, it is this 'throw-away' style that gives *Wuthering Heights* one of its most distinctive qualities, for its Orwellian plainness goes hand-in-hand with a strange and complex story. Professor Daiches called this prose tone 'sublime deadpan', and ascribes to it much of the appeal of the novel. So extraordinary events are narrated in a quite unemotional manner, thus encouraging the reader to accept the story. Possibly this technique is a deliberate ploy, but it is more likely to be instinctive, a true reflection of the essential Emily Brontë. The plain, familiar, 'deadpan' tone of the prose is preferable, perhaps, to the serious, didactic tone of many novels of the Victorian period.

Description is obviously important as a part of the style, and here the author shows the sensitivity we might expect from a life-long poet. Whatever she is describing – a character's appearance or personality, the moors, emotions, domestic items – the prose is strong, flexible, precise, economical, and vividly clear. Occasionally, the description is over-detailed, as in the account of Isabella's feelings and experiences on returning to Wuthering Heights after her marriage, or in the passage dealing with the appearance of the 'house' (1,36–7), though the latter is technically justifiable, because Lockwood is consciously observing and it is the first description the reader gets of a room which sees much of the emotional action.

The temptation to use frequent, long descriptions of the moorland setting must have been great, but here too the author shows restraint and sensitivity – the lyric poet's instinct for simplicity and brevity. The atmosphere of the moors, of nature, is always strong in the story, but the detail evoking it is never excessive. There are many short references to weather and season, and also numerous, economically worded descriptions of various aspects of the moors.

One aspect of the nature descriptions is *sympathetic background* – when events and feelings are given appropriate setting. So we find ghosts active in blizzards (3,54–5) and on rainy nights (34,320); a violent storm marks the death of old Mr Earnshaw and the disappearance of Heathcliff; Cathy's happy birthday excursion is on a 'beautiful spring day' (21,214), but when she is in a sad mood the afternoon 'bodes abundant rain' (22,229); the hero-villain dies on a night of lashing rain (34,318–9); and when Cathy and Hareton combine a reading-lesson with love-making, the weather is suitably idyllic: 'a fragrance of stocks and wall-flowers wafted on the air from amongst the homely fruit-trees.' The convention of 'sympathetic' description has a long history – we see it at work, for instance, in the terrible storm and unnatural happenings that take place on the eve of the assassination in Shakespeare's *Julius Caesar*. More will be said later about this special kind of nature description (see 'Atmosphere and Background').

There is a good deal of conversation in the novel, and much of this is effective: forceful and dramatic. At the high points of the emotional action the dialogue usually transcends the rhetoric of the Gothic tradition and sometimes even attains the impact of Shakespearean blank verse, for the intensities of the emotions are matched by the starkness and urgency of the prose style, as in the important scenes already mentioned in relation to rhythm. Joseph's dialect contributions are often very powerful, for they are accurate, not overfrequent, and reinforce scenes in which their harsh quality is dramatically appropriate (13,155–7, for example). So the heart of the story, as it is reflected in the dialogue, beats strongly, sound as a bell. It is noteworthy also that the author is competent in small but not unimportant technical devices, like avoiding the continual use of 'said' – more specific synonyms like 'hastened to add', 'soliloquized', 'returned', are employed.

Nevertheless, it must be said that much of the conversation lacks spontaneity and naturalness, the characters often speaking in the same 'bookish' style, so that, with the exception of Joseph, there is insufficient differentiation between the various speakers in accordance with their differences in status or personality. There are also lapses into the clichés and overstressing we associate with the language of the Gothic terror tale, and Heathcliff is the main offender, muttering theatrical asides like a stage villain, as, for instance, when he browbeats Isabella (14,164) or terrorizes his son in the 'decoy' episode.

If dialogue is not always successfully handled in the novel, the imagery of the prose is much more impressive. *Wuthering Heights* is a lyrical novel, in the sense that it reflects with concentrated power and sensitivity the writer's very personal view of life and because it is principally concerned with the expression of emotions. It is not surprising, therefore, that such a poetic aspect of the prose style as its imagery should be one of the truest expressions of Emily Brontë's narrative skill. Paradoxically, it may be, much of the language of the story is literal, not figurative, there is very little ornate prose, and the figures of speech are used with characteristic restraint, arising naturally in the flow of prose to illustrate or stress.

There is a strong case for arguing that most of the imagery relates to what is natural rather than human or social – animals, plants, fire, rain, wind, soil, rocks. Some of these recur frequently and so have the force of symbolism: images referring to beasts, fire, wind, rain, food, for example. Parallel with these images deriving from the elemental, animal aspects of life, are those that refer to the supernatural: ghosts, ghouls, vampires, devils; most of these are used to stress either Heathcliff's 'satanic' nature or the spiritual power of the dead Catherine. Since it is clear that the imagery in general is vitally connected to the setting and to the dominant themes and emotions of the novel – love, hatred, revenge, transience, the spiritual power and permanence of nature – it may be called 'thematic' or 'organic', to indicate the difference between it and other, less imaginative figures of speech.

Many other organic images are powerful, intense, and original, illuminating states of body or mind for the most part, and imaginative in the highest sense of the word – a poetic flowering of the prose in brief moments of narrative and descriptive perfection. It is not possible to mention most of these images, but the following are representative. At the very start of the novel, the whole of the setting and tone of the story is evoked in the simile comparing the 'range of gaunt thorns' with beggars 'craving alms of the sun' (1,36). Images of earth, rocks, lightning, and fire suggest the quality of Catherine's passionate affinity with Heathcliff, whereas her feeling for Linton is shown in images of moonbeams, frost, and summer foliage (9,102–4). In Chapter 10, the 'thorn' image is significantly transferred to Catherine, and the Lintons are described as 'honeysuckles embracing the thorn' (10,111–12). Catherine's emotional instability is suggested in the 'gunpowder' metaphor, and her moods are related to alternating sunshine and gloom (10,112).

In the same chapter Heathcliff is, appropriately, 'an arid wilderness of furze and whinstone' (p.121). His violent feelings later erupt in strong, Shakespearean similes: 'crush his ribs in like a rotten hazel-nut', or metaphors: 'Cathy, this lamb of yours threatens like a bull!' (11,132–3). Biblical images turn up from time to time as in the potent sheep/beast metaphor in the last sentence of Chapter 10. Now and then, hyperbole is highly effective (12,142–3, and 14,161). Like Catherine, Heathcliff often uses analogy to contrast his love for the heroine with Edgar's: 'He might as well plant an oak in a flower-pot, and expect it to thrive, as imagine he can restore her to vigour in the soil of his shallow cares!' (14,165). Nature metaphors illuminate the revenge motif: 'And we'll see if one tree won't grow as crooked as another, with the same wind to twist it!' (17,194); Hareton's good qualities struggle to survive like 'good things lost amid a wilderness of weeds' (18,201), or find metaphorical expression in terms of precious metal and common stone: 'one is

gold put to the use of paving-stones', contrasting with Linton's
worthlessness: 'tin polished to ape a service of silver' (21,221).

Finally, it should be noted that, as already suggested (p.106 of
this commentary), the style makes use of symbolism, both in the
recurring imagery and in general; this symbolism has been
noted in relation to other aspects of the novel (see 'Commentaries', 'The characters', and 'Structure'), and will be discussed also in later sections (see 'Themes' and 'Atmosphere and
Background').

Themes and historical and social setting

Themes

Wuthering Heights is such an original, enigmatic novel that it is hardly surprising that there are many different views about its themes – that is, the ideas illustrated by the story. One view is that since Heathcliff is the heart of the story, the theme is an examination of some aspects of evil. Another is that the theme is passionate love and equally violent hatred and revenge; this is perhaps the obvious interpretation. Other critics have suggested that the love of the two chief characters is really mystical, metaphysical, a symbol of the desire for death; for survival after death; of the permanence of the non-human life of nature; of the spiritual craving of the individual for union with this universal 'soul'. Other readers have seen in the 'horror of great darkness' (Charlotte's phrase – see her *Preface*, p.17) that envelops *Wuthering Heights*, the theme of the vanity of human wishes, the transience of life. And there are yet more ideas about the themes – the conflict between the natural and the social life, conflict between different classes, and so on.

It is possible that the truth about the novel's theme is that it is an amalgam of most of these interpretations. Clearly, the theme of love, revealed mainly in the mutual passion of Catherine and Heathcliff, is central. Their passionate love, manifestly physical as well as spiritual, is allowed consummation only in death; in life, it is aborted, and this creates in Heathcliff the destructive passions of bitterness, hate, and vengeance, and in Catherine the destructive conflict that kills her. These dominant themes of thwarted love and manic revenge are, of course, easily related to the central, tragic vision of the novel and the theme of futility – the Ecclesiastesian idea that all is vanity, futility, that, in the words of one of Emily Brontë's favourite literary characters, Macbeth, life 'is a tale/ Told by an idiot, full of sound and fury, / Signifying nothing.'

Perhaps Emily Brontë's primary purpose in her novel is therefore to present an image of life as she understood it, a microcosm, in which the central figure at last regains innocence, his evil elements dissolving in his passionate longing for spiritual union with his lost love. This is the heart of the story, the dominant idea in the author's mysticism, and clear in much of her poetry: that the individual attains happiness only in rare moments of union with God in nature, but returns in death to that ultimate reality. So, like Bunyan's *The Pilgrim's Progress* (another of Emily's favourite books), *Wuthering Heights* may be seen as an allegory: on one level it is a romance concerned with passionate human relationships, but at a deeper level it is concerned with the agonized progress of the human spirit back to the extra-human spirit of which it is a minute part. This is the personal vision that creates the world of *Wuthering Heights*, at once human and mystical, joyous and tormented like her hero and heroine, and giving us both a privileged glimpse into a fascinating mind and a story of unique imaginative power.

Historical and social setting

The story is set in rural Yorkshire in the last forty years of the eighteenth century and the first two of the nineteenth – that is, in the period immediately before the author's own life and therefore similar to it in general circumstances.

Wuthering Heights (see text, Chapter 1, and 'Sources', p.20), usually identified with a farm a few miles from Haworth, is typical of the scattered farmhouses of the moors of the West Riding, but larger. Such farmsteads were durably constructed, with stone floors and huge fire-places – the fire often kept alight in summer as well as winter, and the most common fuel, until the beginning of the nineteenth century, was peat. The farmhouses had small windows, upper rooms accessible more often by ladders rather than staircases, and the occupants kept out weather and intruders alike by means of strong shutters and heavy doors, barred and bolted; and fierce house-dogs were common. The isolated inhabitants discouraged 'foreigners' in self-protection, not unlike primitive tribes. Lighting was candle-powered, and needed constant attention (see Chapter 3, textual notes). In more luxurious residences, like Thrushcross Grange, chandeliers with tapers replaced candles and gave better illumination. In the average farmstead, reading, writing, or household tasks were difficult at night: people tended to retire and rise early, like the birds.

The working day was longer, often with no fixed hours or

holidays. In *Wuthering Heights*, servants and farmworkers are at work before breakfast at harvest time, and a blacksmith shoes a horse after midnight for Heathcliff and Isabella. Social distinctions were very much more marked and rigidly respected: the difference in status between the Earnshaws and the Lintons is clear; there is no question of admitting Heathcliff after the spying episode; Cathy is autocratic towards Hareton whom she thinks a servant (18,200). Servants, especially important ones like Nelly and Joseph, tended to stay in one position all their lives. Roads were poor and few; poor people walked long distances or travelled by horse if they could; the more affluent, like Edgar, journeyed by carriage.

Medicine was a rather primitive business, often using dubious traditional techniques such as bleeding or 'blisters'. Illness was more likely to be fatal or long-lasting – Lockwood spends weeks indoors; fevers of the typhus variety were common and not well understood; 'consumption', not then properly diagnosed as tuberculosis, was a widespread scourge, and usually lethal – Frances, Edgar, Isabella, and Linton all die of it, like Emily herself (The Author's 'Life', p.13). So general expectation of life was shorter. Nutrition was little understood. The principal meals in the farmsteads were breakfast and dinner (at noon).

The law was crude and often ignored in isolated regions. Magistrates were often automatically the important landowners like Edgar; punishments were sometimes disproportionately severe – a thief really could be hanged (see 6,75), and executions were public.

Entertainment was inevitably family-centred (as in the Brontë family itself), consisting for the most part of talk, singing, storytelling and simple games (see 24,245). On special occasions, the local band and choir might visit the principal houses of the area (7,84) – a widespread custom of some antiquity.

Formal education for the poor did not exist: the State system did not get started for another century. If you were well-off, you employed a tutor for your children, as Heathcliff does for Linton – Branwell and Emily's sisters worked as tutors; and there were numbers of small private schools of the kind Charlotte and Emily taught in, where conditions were often far from ideal (Charlotte's *Jane Eyre* contains a bitter picture of Cowan Bridge school, where harshness and injustice hastened the deaths of her two sisters (Author's 'Life', p.13).

Atmosphere and background

As we have already noted (see Author's 'Life', 'Sources', and 'Style'), the physical setting of *Wuthering Heights* is one of its great strengths. The Yorkshire moors are perfectly integrated with theme, events, and characters; like the novels of Thomas Hardy and the 'Barsetshire' novels of Emily's contemporary Trollope, the story is amongst the very best of the so-called 'regional' novels.

Probably the most obvious quality of the moorland background is its vastness and bleakness, its strong winds and rain – at the very beginning, the blizzard that keeps Lockwood overnight at the farmstead establishes the characteristic atmosphere of oppressive power and harshness that we find also in Heathcliff and the house itself. The title of the story is obviously significant in this connection: Wuthering Heights, literally blasted by the north winds, is so often the scene of emotional storms (see 'Style', pp.113–14). The weather is of great importance – from the initial snowstorm to the final rainstorm that accompanies Heathcliff's death. Almost without exception, the chief incidents have a background of weather description, most of which is suitably forbidding: squalls, cold, frost, mist, snow, and so on. As already noted, one of the key images of the landscape is the 'stunted firs' and 'gaunt thorns' near Wuthering Heights. Spring flowers often appear in summer rather than April (22,230); the harvest is normally three weeks later in the Gimmerton region than elsewhere (32,292); the sombre moors are beautiful in summer but dreary or dreadfully inhospitable in winter.

The moors' essential quality of wildness is of course important, and Charlotte Brontë interestingly described her sister's story in terms of its setting: 'moorish, and wild, and knotty as a root of heath' ('Editor's Preface', p.16). This wildness is associated principally with Catherine: she has a strong affinity with the heath, is wild and impulsive in her behaviour, and her favourite occupations are to do with the moors – walking, 'running barefoot', riding. The vitality of the moors is reflected in her vitality, and her daughter inherits this trait in a less violent form. The same energy is found in her love for Heathcliff, in its wildness and power. The wind from the moors is a source of health and vitality both physical and spiritual: in her last illness Catherine yearns for it – 'Do let me feel it – it comes straight down the moor – do let me have one breath!' (12,140). And her creator's mystical passion for the moors is mirrored in Catherine's overwhelming joy when in her dream she is ejected from the orthodox Christian heaven and falls to earth, 'into the middle of the heath on the top of Wuthering Heights' (9,101–2). Also, probably, like the author, Catherine as she approaches death longs for 'escape into that glorious world . . . to be always there: not seeing it dimly through tears, and yearning for it through the walls of an aching heart; but really with it, and in it'. Emily's pantheism is Catherine's less articulate desire for spiritual assimilation into the life of the universe, for union with rocks and trees, wind and heather. In the end it is Heathcliff's yearning too, for union with Catherine means also union with nature in the earth of their graves. The rain on his face and the open window in the death scene (34,318–9) perhaps imply this.

The power, wildness, bleakness and loveliness of the setting combine to make it very real to the reader. Its reality pervades the whole story, helping to suggest the atmosphere of high passion whose appraisal is possibly the main theme of the novel, and also aiding credibility: the basic Gothic tale is so marvellously fused with the most un-Gothic natural background that the sense of realism in the novel is oddly sharp.

As just implied, the personality of Heathcliff (see 'The characters') is one of the most powerful sources of atmosphere. Like the setting itself, his brooding, vengeful nature pervades the story, dominating it as he dominates so many of the people with whom he comes into contact; his personality is as irresistible as a storm. And somehow, owing to his magnetism and complexity he is essentially different from most of the other characters, satanically heroic, a sort of elemental force, generating distinctive feelings of power, violence, fascination, and evil. We seem to be aware of his presence in the story even when he is temporarily absent from the plot – as his son is aware of him on the moor even when he is not actually near. Charlotte called him 'a magnate of the infernal world'; she said also, of the story, that 'in its storm-heated and electrical atmosphere, we seem at times to breathe lightning' ('Editor's Preface', pp.17–18). And this is the kind of atmosphere Heathcliff gives off: the threat of elemental danger. If Edgar's metaphor is 'a fertile valley', Heathcliff personifies the thunder-storm, like the one conjured up by the elements on the night of his disappearance (9,106). In this connection it might be noted that, because of his vital association with the setting, the two nouns that form his mysterious name could well have symbolic force: 'heath' suggests bleakness, strength, romantic wildness, and the word 'cliff' produces an image of terrible danger and, note, is closely related to the word 'abyss', which is used several times in the story to indicate deep grief, loneliness, torment, and suchlike (notably, 16,177). Furthermore, 'cliff' is related, again fancifully perhaps, to 'Heights'. Certainly the moorland where the young Heathcliff roamed in love with his Cathy, or later shot grouse or terrorized his son, is as intimately a part of his personality as it is of Catherine Earnshaw's. It is fitting that the image of the quiet sleepers in the last paragraph of the story should be balanced by the legend of Heathcliff and Cathy haunting the moors: in death as in life it is their most appropriate setting.

It remains only to make a comment on the use of the supernatural in its connection with the atmosphere and background. This has already been discussed throughout the Notes (see 'Sources', p.18; 'Commentaries', pp.28, 45–6, 65, 71–2, 78; 'The characters', pp.82–3, 85–6, 91; 'Structure', pp.103, 105–6, 107–8). It is necessary simply to stress that the supernatural is handled throughout *Wuthering Heights* with subtle dramatic skill, so that it is a source of strangeness, fear, and suspense. It is never crude; even the first sensational apparition figures in Lockwood's nightmare: its ambiguity (is it subjective or objective? – the latter, Heathcliff clearly feels) is somehow appropriate for a ghost. All the other moments suggesting the supernatural through the interaction of past and present and of the various generations, are equally delicate, evoking that suggestion of extra-natural happenings that is one of the fine features of the atmosphere – a good example is when Heathcliff looks into the eyes of the two lovers (33,308). As in Chapter 3, where Lockwood tells us of Heathcliff reacting to his nightmare spectre as if it were real, the last phase of the haunting is described indirectly through brief but intense accounts of the hero's mental and physical response to the spirit he is somehow perceiving. If we too were to see it, as we see Marley's ghost in

Dickens's *A Christmas Carol,* an objective phantom in the sense that it is seen by both Scrooge and the reader, its visual presence would dilute the atmosphere and lessen its ghostliness: phantoms are most frightening when their approach is devious. The passages that deal with the ghost in the last chapter evoke the atmosphere of haunting in the most brilliantly oblique fashion. One of the best of these accounts is (34,315) effective because we *know* that the obsessed Heathcliff sees his beloved's ghost and we too make the imaginative effort, in response to the frightening atmosphere, to see or otherwise sense it (intelligent spectres do not appeal only to our visual sense):

'Now, I perceived he was not looking at the wall; for when I regarded him alone, it seemed exactly that he gazed at something within two yards' distance. And whatever it was, it communicated, apparently, both pleasure and pain in exquisite extremes ... The fancied object was not fixed: either his eyes pursued it with unwearied diligence, and, even in speaking to me, were never weaned away ... if he stretched his hand out to get a piece of bread, his fingers clenched before they reached it, and remained on the table, forgetful of their aim' (34,315).

General questions plus questions on related topics for coursework/examinations on other books you may be studying

1 Account for the popularity of *Wuthering Heights*. (See suggested notes on answer below.)

2 'The action is laid in hell, only it seems places and people have English names there.' Discuss this judgement of *Wuthering Heights*.

3 'The finest merit of the book is that it transforms most of the melodramatic raw material of which it is formed into the stuff of epic narrative of the highest quality.' How far would you agree with this verdict?

4 What, in your opinion, are the chief merits and faults of the novel? Relate your answer to as many of the aspects of the book as possible.

5 'The incredible deeds of incredible people.' Discuss this view of *Wuthering Heights*.

6 'One of Emily Brontë's most extraordinary achievements in this novel is the domiciling of the monstrous in the ordinary rhythms of life and work.' Comment on this statement.

7 *Wuthering Heights* has been called a 'lyrical novel'. Explain what you understand by this term, and show, by means of illustrative references, to what extent you agree with the statement.

8 'The main themes of *Wuthering Heights* are the passions of love and hate and revenge.' Do you agree?

9 Emily Brontë's novel has sometimes been called 'depressing' or 'morbid'. Comment on those aspects of the novel that may have aroused this response, and make clear your own views on the topic.

10 Write a detailed study of Heathcliff, showing the part he plays in the plot and commenting critically on this central character.

11 Discuss Catherine Earnshaw, indicating to what extent she changes in the course of the story and her general importance in the novel.

12 It has been said that after the death of Catherine Earnshaw the rest of the novel is an anti-climax. Do you agree?

13 Comment in detail on the part played by Cathy Linton in the story, referring particularly to (a) her relationships with her two cousins, and (b) to the effect on her of Heathcliff's personality and plans.

14 Write brief character sketches of (a) Linton Heathcliff and (b) Hareton Earnshaw.

15 Discuss the essential differences between Heathcliff and Edgar Linton. How are these revealed in relation to their effects upon Catherine?

16 At one critical point in the novel, Ellen Dean accuses herself of having caused all the misfortunes of her employers. How much truth, if any, would you say is in this idea?

17 Some critics have commented on the improbabilities and coincidences of the novel. Select two or three of these and discuss in some detail their effect upon your own response to the book.

18 Comment on the use of 'multiple narration' in *Wuthering Heights*.

19 Discuss Emily Brontë's use of the supernatural in her novel.

20 Describe critically any two scenes from the novel that reveal (a) pathos, and (b) suspense.

21 Analyse in detail any important scene in the novel, showing its significance for (a) the action, and (b) the themes of the book.

22 Imagine you are *either* a professional critic having to write a review of a novel by 'Ellis Bell', in 1847, *or* a modern critic writing an introduction to a new edition of *Wuthering Heights*. Write an appropriate general comment.

23 Discuss in detail the principal features of Emily Brontë's style in *Wuthering Heights*.

24 Do you consider that Joseph is the most important of the minor characters in the novel? Refer, in your answer, to his nature and function in the story.

25 Discuss the extent to which you think Emily Brontë's own personality and experience may be revealed in her novel.

26 Write an essay on a book you have read where the *setting* is of major importance.

27 Give an account of an unusual and violent character who features in a book you are studying.

28 Outline the characteristics of any two characters in a book you know well who form a contrast with each other.

29 Describe any strange or frightening events in a play or novel or story you have read recently.

30 Give an account of the use of the *unexpected* in any novel you have read.

31 Write about the use of the *first-person* ('I') narrator in a book you have read.

32 In what ways is *nature* important in any *two* of the books you have read.

33 Describe the part played by a servant in a book you have studied.

Suggested notes for essay answer to question one:

1 Introduction (one paragraph):
W.H. popular because it is a good story; define 'good story' (clear plot, interesting characters, credible setting, realistic dialogue, strong structure, effective style, important themes – the whole somehow coming to life owing to the general narrative skill).
Added fascination of the 'Brontë story': Emily one of four gifted children, all poets and novelists, all doomed to premature death; their literary fantasy world when young; later publications.

2 The attractive features of the plot (one or more paragraphs): clear-cut – no irrelevant/confusing complications – give brief synopsis only, to indicate clarity – do not 'tell the story'; dramatic interest of the emotional conflicts – between Heathcliff and Hindley, Heathcliff and Edgar etc.; fascination of the supernatural element.

3 Powerful central interest of the characters (two or more paragraphs): Heathcliff's dominance and complexity: 'Gothic' but also psychologically credible – his motives and typical behaviour; Catherine: intrinsic interest as credible/attractive person – her dilemma, reflected in her love for two very different men; other interesting characters: Nelly, Cathy, Hindley, Joseph, etc. – be specific about *why* they are colourful: e.g. religiosity and dialect in Joseph, adolescent desire for love in Cathy, and her impulsive warmth, Nelly's charming matter-of-factness, Hindley's resentment of the 'cuckoo', his violence and vindictiveness.
N.B. Naturally you do not have to 'like' characters to find them interesting: Heathcliff is obviously villainous, but since he is magnetic he is necessarily interesting.

4 The interest of the setting (one paragraph): powerful source of atmosphere, relation to characters/themes etc.; autobiographical interest of the Yorkshire moors – Emily's own 'setting'.

5 The attractive features of the construction (one or more paragraphs): popular saga element – long family history; clever use of 'multiple narration', e.g. in integrating the various generations; balance of opposites – the 'monstrous' and the 'ordinary' etc.; the lyrical action of the emotional crises; the blending of the melodramatic traits of the Gothic romance with powerful narrative originality.

6 The many appealing qualities of the style: clarity, forcefulness, fluency, effective imagery, absence of authorial intrusiveness, etc. (One or more paragraphs).

7 Popularity also depends upon the fact that the themes of the novel are those that do not date – the so-called 'eternal verities': love, birth, death, the struggle to survive, spiritual aspirations, weaknesses and evils such as hate and revenge. (One or more paragraphs.)

8 Brief paragraph to sum up: *W.H.* therefore is an arrestingly interesting story, many-faceted, and appealing both to those who like romantic themes and plots, and in more original, subtle ways to those able to respond to great literature.

(These suggestions for answering question 1 are, of course, guidelines only: they may be varied in any reasonable way, and do not constitute a comprehensive body of ideas.)

N.B. In answering such questions it is important to avoid simply 'telling the story', to ensure that your essay is clearly relevant, and to provide adequate suitable references and brief quotations to illustrate your answer.

Further reading

Cecil, Lord David: *Early Victorian Novelists* (Chapter 5), 1948. OP.

Daiches, David: Introduction to the Penguin Edition of *Wuthering Heights*, 1965.

Drabble, Margaret: Introduction to *Wuthering Heights and Poems*, Everyman Paperback, 1978.

Gérin, Winifred: *Emily Brontë, a biography*, Oxford Paperback, 1978.

Kettle, Arnold: *An Introduction to the English Novel*, Hutchinson Educational: Unwin Hyman 1967, vol. 1, part 3, 1951.

Klingopulos, G.D.: 'The Novel as Dramatic Poem', *Scrutiny*, XIV, 4, 1947.

Moser, Thomas C.: *Wuthering Heights: Text, Sources, Criticism*, Harbrace Sourcebook, 1962:

Spark, Muriel and Stanford, Derek: *Emily Brontë, Her Life and Work*, Arrow Books, 1985.

Van Ghent, Dorothy: 'On *Wuthering Heights*', in *The English Novel: Form and Function*, 1953, 1961. ?OP.